CW01496332

Long Stays in
SPAIN

Long Stays in
SPAIN

A COMPLETE, PRACTICAL GUIDE TO
LIVING AND WORKING IN SPAIN

PETER DAVEY

HIPPOCRENE
BOOKS, INC.

DAVID & CHARLES
Newton Abbot London

HIPPOCRENE BOOKS
New York

British Library Cataloguing in Publication Data

Davey, Peter
  Long stays in Spain.
  1. Spain – Visitors' guides
  I. Title
  914.6'0483

  ISBN 0-7153-9494-0

Printed in Great Britain
by Billing and Son Worcester
for David & Charles plc
Brunel House Newton Abbot Devon

Published in the United States of America
by Hippocrene Books Inc
171 Madison Avenue
New York NY10016

Contents

Acknowledgements

This book has been compiled from information and personal experiences gathered over a period of twelve years whilst both visiting and living in Spain.

To mention all of the people who have contributed would be quite impossible, thus it is with some difficulty that I have singled out the individuals and agencies who have helped during the actual writing of the book.

The Spanish Consulate's office in London have been particularly helpful with their fact sheets, guides and the personal service at their office near Sloane Square.

Peter and Silvia Blackmore of Son Font for their help on the buying and selling of a property. Antonio Pujol Cortes and his wife Freda for an insight into many aspects of Spanish life. Francisco Garau Bauza of the Banco de Bilbao. Beatriz Arnau Gutierrez and Reyes Carpintero Gonzalez for their help with the section on Cantabria. Antonio Mir for his stories about Spanish history and bullfighting. Alan and Nancy Pujol and Pau Alberti Salamanca for their help with sport and the Spanish educational system. Barrie Wiggins of the Baleares International School for his help with the section on English schools in Spain. Schembri (Palma) helped on car importing. Jeff and Gill Quirk of BPS for their help with work and business permits. The Rev Frank Millar for his help with the English Church section. Jackie Picket de Segeu for her help with tourism. Centro de Gestion Catastral and Hacienda Palma for their help with taxes and property transfer. Ayuntamiento de Calvia on the mysteries of urban *contribucion*. Colin and Jill Hall who flew out with a new typewriter when ours gave up. And finally the Guardia Civil and Municipal Police Departments who helped with the section on crime and traffic law.

Introduction

Spain is a country of contrasts, spreading in diverse majesty from the foothills of the Pyrenees in the north to the straits of Gibraltar in the south, and from the Atlantic in the west to the Mediterranean in the east. It has a documented history that is second to none and its equitable climate has done much to preserve its historical buildings and sites. In Spain you can never be bored: there is always something worth seeing going on somewhere – a *fiesta*, a fair, a pilgrimage, a seasonal celebration, all of which help to enhance the differentness of this attractive country.

It is also a country of recent change: when Generalissimo Francisco Franco died in 1975, political reform was sweeping, moving away from repressive dictatorship to a democratic constitutional monarchy under King Juan Carlos and Queen Sofia. In 1976 the constitution was altered by referendum, and in 1977 the first free elections for 40 years were held: the socialists gained power immediately, together with the centre party – a strong judgement on Franco's right-wing groups. It is against this background that we see Spain's greatest changes taking place: laws on divorce, abortion and contraception are now being given government approval; the working man's interests are now protected by far-reaching laws on work contracts; and a mini-welfare state is emerging with cradle-to-the-grave care for those who cannot manage for themselves.

It is a slow process, and many of the changes are not welcomed by the older Spanish people who see them as a movement away from the church and its teachings. Materialism did indeed prevail and the particularly Spanish *el destape* – the literal translation being 'uncovering' – led to a relaxation of censorship: *Playboy* magazines and the like started to appear on the news-stands, slightly risqué girlie shows were staged in resort clubs, topless girls appeared on the beaches, and many nudist camps and beaches were established. Cheap food, drink and accommodation have brought an ever-increasing band of tourists to the country each year for the sun, the sand and the wine. That number now reaches a staggering 54 million each year, and in addition there are over 1.3 million foreign property owners who either live here permanently or come with their families and friends at least once a year.

It is therefore small wonder that Spain is in a state of change. She has also recently become an active member of the EC, with all the benefits and responsibilities that this may or may not bring when the trade barriers are lifted in January 1993. She, too, has a NATO (OTAN) commitment, with American air bases established on her soil. Furthermore, there is still the ongoing conflict with the UK over the sovereignty of Gibraltar, with its occasional border squabbles. All in all, if you go to Spain for a long stay, it is essential to be as well informed about the country as you can; by keeping up with current events you should gain a much better understanding of this fascinating country and its people.

This book is but a 'taster', and has been written expressly to help those people contemplating a long stay or period of residence, to guide them through the maze of paperwork and bureaucratic difficulties they may encounter. The information given in the text has been checked and was correct at the time of going to press, but like all things in Spain regulations can change from day to day and from region to region, so check at the Spanish Consulate if you have doubts before you leave; the delegates are charming people who are usually very helpful. Once you have arrived in Spain, you will find groups of British people throughout the country who will provide a fund of current information about the local laws and taxes that prevail in your chosen area. What else is there to talk about when you don't have the vagaries of climate any more as a staple topic for conversation?

1
Why Spain?

A recent survey carried out by a property management group estimated that there were over 1.3 million properties owned by foreigners in Spain, and this is being added to at an ever-increasing rate each year. Inevitably one wonders who is buying, and why?

Anyone who has visited the Spanish Consulate in London recently will realise that a large percentage of would-be settlers are from the UK. The enquiries office is always full of people and there is now a special telephone number (071-581-5925) with a long recorded message covering the questions most frequently received.

Tourism in the early sixties coupled with increasing affluence gave people a taste of Mediterranean life; this was to have a bad effect on Spain's building development, however. At that time properties were cheap but scarce, and Spain was quick to recognise this deficit; she immediately embarked upon a series of cheap high-rise developments which were poorly constructed and badly sited. Magalluf on Mallorca was a typical example, though happily there are now schemes afoot to demolish much of the unsightly construction and replace it with an inland marina. However, as these properties were so cheap, and as it took so little time and money to reach them (the return flight from Gatwick in the sixties was around £20), people bought as fast as the builders built. But services did not keep up with developments, and it became more attractive for foreigners to enlist the aid of Spanish partners and open bars or cafés, and in that way cream off some of the profits being made in the new sunny Klondike.

By the early seventies legislation arrived to save many coastal regions from ruination; the mass of tourists seeking cheap holidays were therefore crammed into a few densely populated areas which were by then already saturated with bars, cafés, discos, hire-car firms and the like, many run by foreigners. Competition was high and people worked long hours to stay competitive, though many had to admit defeat and went back home. There was a lull in development; in the UK, stringent economic measures were applied in the form of the dollar premium whereby her citizens could take only limited funds abroad without the penalty of extra taxes. Development in Spain slowed and local governments had time to study more satisfactory ways to utilise their new-found wealth. Planning offices were set up and building regulations were more strictly applied. 'Low-rise' became the developers' slogan, and tasteful villa complexes (*pueblos*) were started whose central theme comprised fountains, swimming pools, tennis courts and – in the more expensive areas – golf courses.

The dollar premium was lifted in 1977 and the boom resumed, but this time with a slightly more discerning buyer. Letting agencies offered a guaranteed income for those who only used their properties for part of the year. Increasing affluence on the part of the British, bolstered by the North Sea oil boom with its resulting strong pound, made second and third holidays a distinct possibility and it was far nicer to spend them in a place of your own in the sun. Early retirement coupled with index-linked pensions gave confidence to many retired people who in earlier days might have feared the loss of spending power of their fixed pensions.

Since Spain has joined the EC, regulations regarding work permits and residence have been easing as 1992/3 draws near. Many professional people – doctors, nurses, teachers, financial consultants and accountants as well as builders, carpenters, plumbers, electricians and boat chandlers – have arrived to augment the established bar-owners, hire-car firms and restaurant owners.

We can therefore conclude that people come for two basic reasons: to retire cheaply and in comfort, or to make money. In the following chapters you will be able to assess for yourself how right they are to do so, but suffice it to say that Spain is cheaper to live in than the UK or the USA, and its climate is certainly more equable. Fortunes can be made by the enterprising, too, but competition is high and success only comes to the few who have the bright ideas and the strength to carry them out, particularly in the face of an antiquated bureaucratic system that protracts everything, apparently on principle.

Geography

Spain is roughly twice as large as Britain, over 500 miles (805km) north–south and 550 miles (885km) east–west, and because of its size and its position separating, as it were, the Atlantic from the Mediterranean, it has a widely varying climate. The summer visitor might well imagine a land where the sun shines continuously and rain is an infrequent caller. This is not so, however; Spain experiences both regions of near-desert conditions, as well as regions with almost daily rainfall. In addition, the geology of Spain results in a variety of micro-climates, since its mountain ranges effectively block rain and wind: thus the Pyrenees absorb much of the harshness of Europe's winter, and the Cantabrian mountains to the west cause unusually high rainfall as Atlantic clouds rise to pass over them. Yet the central plateau region is almost desert-like for much of the year, with hot summers and icy winters. It is therefore difficult to describe each region in detail, so we will simply give the would-be settler an idea of the generally prevailing influences of each area.

In general there are four main climatic zones. The most north-westerly area is dominated by the mild, wet influence of the Atlantic, and encompasses the regions of Galicia, Cantabria, Vascongadas and Asturias. Winters are cold and wet, and summers warm and humid with misty rains dominating sometimes for days on end. Temperatures range from 45° to 59°F (7° to 15°C) in winter and from 52° to 77°F (11° to 25°C) in summer. Annual

11

rainfall is from around 35in (900mm) to 47in (1,200mm) spread over 150–200 days with up to 2,400 sun hours.

To the north-east lies the Pyrenean region of Navarra and Aragon which is slightly drier and less mild in winter – snow is a frequent visitor and blocked roads can cause chaos after exceptional falls; summer temperatures are up to 80°–86°F (27°–30°C) in July and August with little rainfall at that time; there are up to 2,600 sun hours.

To the south, and extending to the great mountain ranges of the Sierra Morena and Sierra Nevada, is the central continental zone of the high plateau of 'Meseta'. At an average altitude of 984–3,280ft (300–1,000m), the dry harsh terrain has the classical appearance featured in many spaghetti westerns. Winters are icy cold with dramatically low night temperatures, summers are hot and arid with only sparse rainfall and with some 2,700–3,000 sun hours in the year. Winter temperatures average from -4°F (-20°F) minimum to 52°F (11°C) maximum, and summer ones from 64° (18°C) to 104°F (40°C) plus; the rainfall average is a meagre 12in (300mm) over 40–55 days.

To the south of the Sierra Nevada the climate of the Costa del Sol is unique: shielded by her mountain ranges, it produces 2,900–3,000 sun hours per annum, and 16in (400mm) rainfall over 60–70 days, though less than 1 per cent of this in summer when the temperatures range from 68°F (20°C) to 104°F (40°C). Winter temperatures range from 48°F (9°C) to 68°F (20°C).

Finally there is the Mediterranean climate of Spain's lengthy eastern seaboard: the figures for Valencia, halfway down the coast, may be used as a guide with winter temperatures ranging from 45°F (7°C) to 61°F (16°C) and summer ones from 66°F (19°C) to 95°F (35°C); rainfall averages 12–27in (300–700mm) over 80 days with some 3,000 plus sun hours. The Balearic Islands are included in this range.

All the figures given are very much averaged out from data gathered over five or six years; it is quite impossible to lay down information which can give an accurate guide as to what one may expect in any given year. During this past winter, for instance (1988/9), large tracts of northern Spain suffered torrential rain and snow storms which lasted for many weeks – but these were just as out of character as were the hurricane-force winds which swept through the southern UK in 1987.

A Potted History

Serious students of Spanish history should now move on to another chapter, because all one may do in a book of this nature is to give a brief outline of events leading up to the country's present state of being a constitutional monarchy with a socialist government.

Firm evidence of regular human settlement in the Spanish peninsula can be traced back to 4,000BC when Neolithic man cultivated the coastal region of the Levante and left his mark in his burial grounds and ditch systems.

From about 1,000 to 900BC the Phoenicians were setting up their trading settlements on southern Spain's Mediterranean coast; at the same time the Celts were moving into the northern regions and finally, after forays to the south, settled in the Cantabrian coastal regions around Galicia and Asturias. The Carthaginians fought and had finally dominated the whole of southern Spain by around 500BC; they maintained their hold until they in their turn were defeated by the Romans in 217BC. The Romans fought through southern Spain until all resistance was quelled; their final thrust northwards in 19BC gave them the Cantabrian regions, with only the Basques being left as a pocket of resistance in their difficult mountain territory. By the fifth century AD the Roman Empire was in decline, and the Visigoths who had been fighting alongside the Romans were left with overall power in Spain; they established their capital in Toledo. The Romans had introduced Christianity by this time, and from thenceforward a Christian-dominated society grew throughout Spain.

In the eighth century the Moorish army of Muslims

13

marched into southern Spain, and in nine years had conquered most of the country and its people with the exception of the Celtic Christians who took refuge in their mountain regions of the north. By the early twelfth century the ephemeral warring between Christians and Muslims had ceased, and by peaceful means the majority of the northern half of Spain was once again practising Christianity.

The fifteenth and sixteenth centuries saw the rise of the Catholic monarchs, and it was in the late fifteenth century that the infamous Inquisition carried out its purging of the Jewish population, when thousands were deported.

The ensuing years saw the rise and decline of Spain as a world power: great explorers sailed the seas, to be followed by armies who captured lands in the name of Spain and brought back gold and jewels as well as many of the fine fruits and vegetables we see on our market stalls today. 1588 saw the disastrous defeat of the Armada, which was brought about as much by bad weather and chaotic leadership as by English seamanship; the final maritime blow was delivered by Nelson at the Battle of Trafalgar in 1805.

There followed a long period of unrest – internal strife and revolt by Spain's provinces further weakened her world standing, and culminated in the loss of most of her overseas territories as well.

Spain was first declared a republic in 1873, but she was still a nation divided; it wasn't until 1931 that the second republic was established. However, further unrest followed and in 1936 the civil war began, triggered off by a military uprising led by one General Franco. The war ended in 1939 with victory to Franco: he established a harsh dictatorship with no quarter given to those who transgressed; during World War II he declared Spain neutral but gave tacit and active support to the Axis forces.

Franco died in 1975; he had already decreed that upon his death a constitutional monarchy should be established with Juan Carlos I as King, and in the years that followed democratic government was therefore set up: each region with a specific identity was given autonomous status, with their responsibility to central government.

The current socialist government led by Prime Minister Felipe Gonzalez has been in power since 1982. The economy is stable, and Spain is now enjoying the benefits of her entry into the EC in 1986.

1 January 1993 represents the next milestone in her history, and everyone waits with baited breath to see how the relaxation of cross-border regulations will be interpreted in this country where everything bureaucratic is slightly different.

An Outline of Spanish Government

As in the UK, after an election the king asks the leader of the winning party to form a government; there is an independent judiciary, and the administration is divided into autonomous regions, provinces and municipalities.

Each autonomous region has its own elected parliament and administration funded by central government; their powers are similar to those exercised by the large conurbations in the UK and cover cradle-to-grave social responsibilities, also development, tourism and public works. Each region has its own capital and flag, and the Basque region has its own police force.

Recent European Parliamentary elections have resulted in a markedly socialist contingent being sent to Brussels to represent Spain's interests.

Autonomous regions of Spain

2
People and Places

Spain is known to have been inhabited by man since around 25,000BC, the date ascribed to the famous cave drawings in Altamira, Cantabria. Her total population now is around 39 millions, but since nearly two-thirds live in a handful of major cities and industrial regions there are vast areas in the central region which are only sparsely populated. The total area of Spain is about twice that of Britain.

As already discussed, Spain, like Britain, has a long and varied history of occupation by many invading armies; in their turn Phoenicians, Moors, Greeks and Romans have left their mark on the Spanish countryside and its people. It is therefore debatable whether the tall, aqualine, olive-skinned, brown-eyed dancer is any more representative of the typical Spaniard than the fair-haired blue-eyed Westcountryman is representative of the typical Englishman.

Also like England, Spain once had a very successful adventuring force which by the sixteenth century could claim for her flag Naples and the low countries of Europe as well as Central and South America and the Philippines; quite rightly, Spain boasted that the sun never set on Spanish soil, and she left her mark overseas not only in language but in her religion and architecture, too. It is possibly because of this background of global influence that the Spanish mien is still typified by a certain 'presence', an air of authority which is best seen in their dancing and posturing bullfighters. To the unenlightened the Spanish can appear cold and reserved, when in fact they are merely behaving correctly according to their own customs. Hopefully this book will help you appreciate that this sense of formality should not be taken as aloofness, but accepted as part of a culture where in fact considerable respect is shown for one's fellow men. Spain is quite different from the rest of Europe; she is only just emerging into the democratic world, and it is a slow process – and not all of the changes that are being made are for the good. Mobility and the new-found freedom threaten the family ties which have been the cornerstone of the Spanish way of life for centuries, and many old Spaniards are far from happy about that.

The Regions
The Basque Region
This is by far the oldest historically and its people are the least changed; it encompasses the provinces of Guipuzcoa, Viscaya and Alava in Spain, and the Basques themselves also claim the area known to them as the 'Pirineosbujos', extending into the French Pyrenees. Their language, 'Vascuence', is of unknown origin and is completely unlike any other European language. It is thought that these people are direct descendants of the original inhabitants of the peninsula who during early occupations in the centuries BC were driven back by the invading Phoenicians, Celts and Carthaginians to this north-west stronghold on the Biscay mountain shore, where they have remained ever since. There is some scientific evidence to support this theory, too, in their physical likeness and similarity of blood grouping.

The Basques are fiercely patriotic, and have long sought complete autonomy – at times violently – through their militant faction ETA who have been responsible for a wave of shootings and bombings throughout Spain. They have long memories, too, and recall only too well Franco's action on 26 April 1937 of summoning his allies, the Nazi Condor Legions, to bomb and destroy the town of Guernica during the civil war – the town was the seat of Basque local government, dating back to the fourteenth century. There is now a shrine in the town dedicated to the 2,000

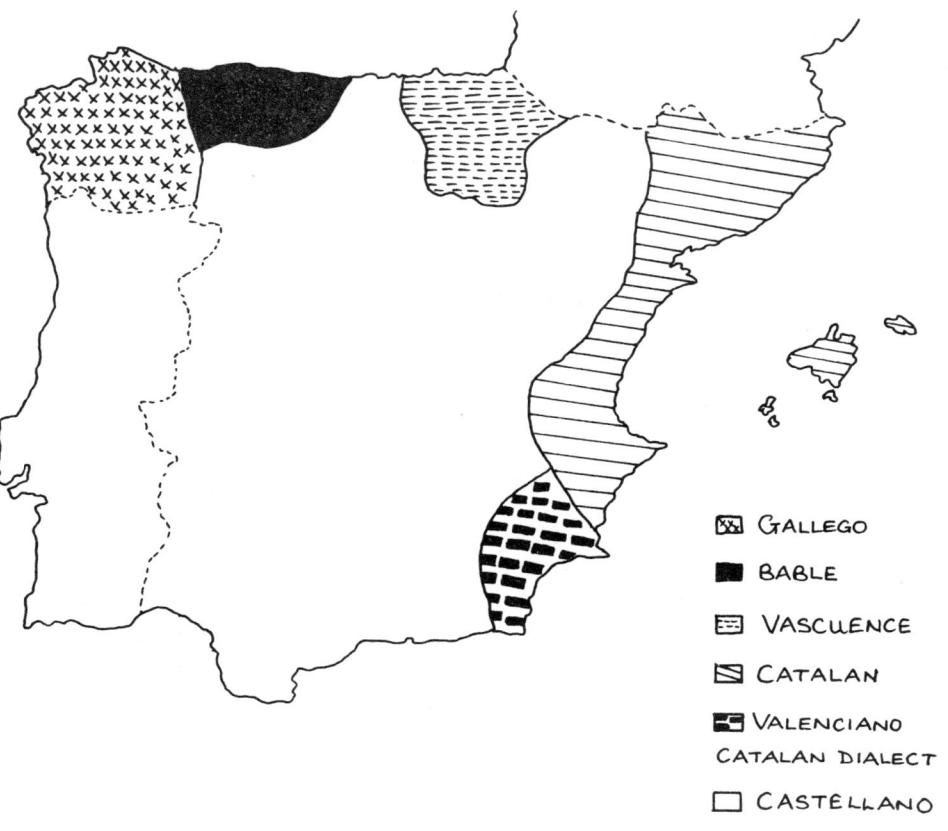

GALLEGO

BABLE

VASCUENCE

CATALAN

VALENCIANO
CATALAN DIALECT

CASTELLANO

Linguistic divisions

people who perished; however, there is no greater tribute than Picasso's masterpiece 'Guernica' which hangs in a Madrid museum.

There is an attempt at dialogue even now, the terrorists having undertaken to cease hostilities whilst talks go on. But even as I write this truce has broken down and another wave of bombings and killings has started. The region contains much of Spain's industrial wealth and mines, so it is difficult to see how a compromise will ever be reached because of the economic ramifications.

Not all the Basques work in mines or factories; a large section are cattle herders and follow the ancient nomadic principles of moving up into high mountain pastures with their herds of sheep, goats and cows in the spring, and returning to the valleys for the winters. They make excellent cheeses whilst living in their mountain retreats, and these are a delicacy much sought-after by those who frequent the Cantabrian coastal region for their holidays.

Aragon
Aragon extends from the foothills of the Pyrenees to its capital Zaragoza in the south, and is a region of contrasts; this geographical location results in an irregular rainfall and thus does little to compete with the agrarian way of life seen further to the west where the rains are more reliable. However to the north, fast-flowing rivers and streams wend their way down from the Pyrenean snow-melt zones, and in this region deciduous trees abound – the Cerdesa National Park is one of Spain's largest protected areas of conservation and is host to both skiers in the winter and campers in the summer. From Jaca northwards, a spectacular mountainous countryside opens up, its snow-capped peaks an almost permanent backdrop. Wildlife abounds, and many species of flora and fauna are unique to this area.

Historically, Aragon was on the route taken by the pilgrims as they moved from Europe to Santiago de Compostela – they entered Spain through Aragon's northern mountain pass at Somport. Much of the art in this region is considered to have been influenced by these early visitors as they plied their crafts along the route.

Catalonia

To the east is Catalonia, also with its own language, 'Catalan', and with its own, though less strident call for autonomy. The Catalans are thought to be descended from the people who in the Middle Ages settled in the Gulf of Lyons area in the south of France, and were driven west by invading armies. In Franco's day Catalan language classes were held in secret as it was a banned language during his dictatorship. Nowadays they fare better: under the current moderate socialist government they have one national and one regional television station of their own, and a host of local radio stations all broadcasting in Catalan. Road signs, public signs and notices are in both Catalan and Castilliano, although the graffiti artists are doing their level best to obliterate the latter.

Catalonia is altogether a prosperous region. Barcelona is its principal city with two million inhabitants; it is also the home of such industrial giants as the Seat car manufacturers, and many ceramic and chemical-producing factories. There is plenty of both light and heavy industry in the region, which is served by rail and motorway to the west and Barcelona harbour to the east. Catalonia has the good fortune to possess varied assets so she can diversify in her economic structure: to the north are the Spanish Pyrenean ski resorts, and to the east the Costas Dorada and Brava – the influx of workers from all parts of Spain to this region in itself underlines its importance and its economic stability.

The Balearics

Further to the east the Balearics bloom from the sea like golden flowers. For years they were the holiday islands of the rich only – now they are accessible to all, in a short two-hour flight to enjoy the sun, sand, sea and sangria which seem to satisfy the needs of so many;

and Palma airport handles more passengers in a day in high season than many of our provincial airports do in a year. It is the holiday industry, therefore, that rules here. Nonetheless these islands have a long history; they also possess a unique flora and fauna which make them a biologist's dream.

The Mallorquins, too, have a language of their own – it has only been transcribed in recent years and appears to be a mixture of Catalan and French, the French having had a considerable influence on the northern seaboard of Mallorca where an established fishing community was formed. Many place-names and locally used words bear the mark of the French presence.

Because of the prosperity of the holiday trade many mainland Spaniards come to work on the islands. Surprisingly they are called *foresteros* (strangers) and are not welcomed by the locals who believe that they syphon back to the mainland all the money they make; in fact, they are far less tolerated than the *extranjeros* (foreigners) who by contrast bring money *to* the islands.

Currently the islands are seeing a time of great change, and wildlife preservationists fight tooth and nail with the marina developers and complex builders. It is a time for prosperity and development, but also a time to change sullied images, to try to attract the more discerning who will to a greater extent appreciate the history and beauty of islands the population considers are jewels in the ocean.

The Levente
On the mainland and to the south of Catalonia lies the Levente or Valencian region; Valencia is the capital, and the language spoken is a mixture of Castillian and a local form of Catalan. There has been a great influx of Spaniards from other regions over the past decade and currently the population stands at some four million.

This is the major food-producing region of Spain, with crops ranging from vegetables to fruit and rice; much of it is exported both to other parts of Spain and to Europe where it earns valuable foreign currency. Like Catalonia, there is plenty of diversification in the economy; on the Mediterranean shores there are relatively new and tasteful developments of the Costa Blanca – Alicante, Calpe and Dania with their marinas, golf courses and low-rise chalet *pueblos* are much favoured by the more discerning foreign settler.

In Valencia itself there are thriving furniture-producing factories which supply both Spain's ever-increasing demand and also export to Europe, mostly in flat-pack, do-it-yourself models at very competitive prices. Valencian wine is both good and cheap, and provides house wines for both Spain and abroad. And it would be remiss not to mention the Falles, Valencia's most famous *fiesta*; traditionally it culminates in fireworks and the burning of the effigies, and always attracts people from all over Spain and even some from Europe. It is said that you must book your own room for the next Falles as you leave the current one – otherwise you don't get in, such is its popularity.

Andalucia
Andalucia is the region which comes most readily to mind when people think of Spain. Its Flamenco dancers and singers, its unique style of guitar-playing with heavy base melody and strumming, its bull fights, sherry, and the grand architecture of its principal towns and cities – all these conjure up the text-book image that movie-makers have reinforced throughout the past two decades or so. Their fiestas are frenetic affairs, as befits the climate and a people for whom the summer goes on and on.

In hortological terms Andalucia quite rightly carries the title of 'the greenhouse of Europe' and to extend what is already a long growing season market gardeners have erected acre upon acre of polythene tunnels to gather a year-round harvest of tomatoes, lettuce, cucumber and strawberries. This compulsion to provide endless crops may stem from an historical background of alternate glut and famine dictated by the vagaries of the annual rainfall in times past.

Throughout Spain the typical Andalucian is traditionally regarded as rather vain and attention-seeking, though this image may have been generated by those envious of a land of sunshine and stability with its people who like gaiety and humour. The Andalucian's singing stems from his gypsy roots and the songs of the harvest workers; to the untrained ear it seems to have a rather repetitive element, with sudden rises and falls in volume which takes one quite by surprise.

The economy of the area is extremely stable with the rich resorts of the Costa del Sol to the south, the vast business and commercial centres of Cadiz, Cordoba, Granada and Sevilla, not to mention the world-famous wine and sherry region Jerez de la Frontera with its unique *bodegas* and long tradition of *fiestas*. Further up the coast are the coastal resorts without which no holiday brochure is complete: Fuengirola, Estepona, Malaga, Torremolinos to name but a few, places where tourists congregate in the summer in their hundreds of thousands. It is the home of *paella* and chips, of tea like mother makes, and of high-rise developments which resemble more the bad aspects of Miami beach than they do Spain. However, these resorts do provide cheap sunshine holidays for many who would not otherwise be able to afford a holiday at all – the cost of a visit here by a family prepared to rent a self-catering flat can work out a lot cheaper than going to Devon or Cornwall, and the weather is foolproof. They also provide a guaranteed input of valuable foreign currency to help keep Spain's economy stable.

The Meseta
It is not possible in a book of this type to cover every region, so the central Meseta area of Extramadura, Castilla la Nueva, Leon and part of Castilla la Vieja must be considered together. By far the greater part of this arid table land is inhabited by Castillians who have given their name to

the worldwide spoken Spanish language 'Castilliano', and who are a people of tremendous resource and ambition. They were caricatured to excess by Cervantes in his 'Don Quixote' who carried all of their virtues to the extreme.

Outside the major cities, this vast plateau is sparsely populated, the windmills and rocky outcrops somehow striking a balance with the castles, cathedrals, monasteries and other buildings of arresting architecture which pepper the region and the capital Madrid. And who else but the Spanish would put their major city in the exact heart of their land? Its 3.2 million inhabitants freeze in the winter and swelter in summer, such is the effect of living in a central table land. But it is said that all roads lead to Madrid, and as far as bureaucratic routine is concerned you will soon believe it – Madrid is the administrative centre for the whole of Spain, and anything worth signing must be counter-signed there. Not only is it the centre of commerce: it is also the seat of government, and its power base wields the final sanction over Spain's many autonomous regions. It is the home of the Spanish royal family, and the treasure house of much of Spain's vast collection of works of art.

In the surrounding region are such thought-provoking place-names as Toledo, Salamanca, Segovia and Avila, centres of artistic tradition as well as commercial cities in their own right.

The Costa Verde
Galicia, Asturias and the Cantabrian coast; this northwestern area is one of great contrast, which recently has seen much economic and political change, too. Known as the Costa Verde (Green Coast) it includes the regions of Galicia, Asturias and part of Castilla la Vieja (Old Castile). Asturias holds the middle ground and was once a kingdom in its own right; and it is still said that to be King of Spain you must first be the Prince of Asturias.

Forming a natural barrier between this region and the rest of Spain are the Cantabrian mountains with the famous Picos de Europa rising to 8,500ft (2,600m). This is an area of outstanding beauty with great tracts set aside as national parkland. Brown bears and wild goats still roam its hillsides, and high above flies the enigmatic eagle – called the 'bone-breaker' because it survives largely on a diet of bones which it drops from a height to shatter upon the rugged scree slopes. One wonders how it finds the splinters, let alone how its digestive system works once they are swallowed.

Hikers and naturalists are drawn to this region every year as the beaches of the Atlantic shores have long been favoured by the more discerning Spaniards.

Whilst it is the green coast, it is also the grey smog-laden coast: in Asturias are found Spain's main coal and iron-ore resources, inevitably accompanied by the smelters for steel and heavy manufacturing plant. It is also an area of political unrest, and it is said that communism has a good foothold in many of the factories, mines and ship-building yards. Like other northern regions it does have a language of its own but again, as so many early languages, it has not been able to keep up with the times and is now considerably modified with Castilliano and other tongues.

Because of its north-westerly aspect facing the Atlantic, this is a region known and revered for its fishermen and fish dishes. The Cantabrian fleets ply as far away as Iceland and the Grand Banks of Canada, and the cooks of the region deal proudly with their catches. The Picos de Europa region also produces cheeses which are unique, traditionally hand-crafted by mountain villagers in ways handed down from one generation to another; because of the small number of people involved in the craft, output is very low and the production of these cheeses is both expensive and extremely limited.

The climate of this whole region is mild and wet, and has by far the highest rainfall in Spain. Lush pastures feed fine herds of cattle, sheep and goats, and Cantabrian dairy produce is dispatched to all parts of Spain, particularly the drought-ridden central and southern regions. The milk is given UHT treatment which preserves its freshness for many months.

The Spanish Way of Life

In principle the time of change for Spain started around the early 1960s; at this time she experienced a period of economic transformation, helped not only by aid from more well-off nations but by the rapid rise in the level of her industry and tourism which brought in much-needed foreign currency with which she could finance further schemes. Franco had been in power for 36 years when he died in 1975 and his dictatorship ended: suddenly there was freedom of speech, the press came to life, and for the first time in living memory an opposition party was allowed to stand. Then in November 1975 Juan Carlos of Borbon was proclaimed king. The effect these changes brought about had far-reaching consequences upon the very substance of Spanish life – the rigidity was gone overnight as it were, and the new-found liberty left people rather stunned. Even daily life saw changes as people entered a more hedonistic era and were carried along with the country's new-found wealth. Today, therefore, we see a Spain in change. As the demands of work mobility have developed, so the strong family ties have gone; now there are more nuclear family groups, isolated from what were once very supportive extended family ties. Some of the old elements do, however, still exist – visiting the family is still high on the list of the things one does at weekends and fiestas, and grandmothers still provide a helping hand where they can to care for the young offspring of working mothers.

Of necessity mealtimes have changed as the Spanish working day has had to adapt to the working day of industry and tourism – tourists bring their mealtimes with them. Nowadays, that delightfully long lunch which was usually taken between 2 and 4pm in the afternoon and followed by a siesta has all but disappeared, except for the lucky few who enjoy it at weekends. However, in the more central, rural and small-town areas, away from the influences of tourism and industry, the traditional Spanish way of life and eating habits can still be observed.

Breakfast (*el desayuno*) is a very light meal of coffee, toast, and croissants, and *ensaimadas* or *churros* – cooked, sweet flour mixtures, light and fluffy.

Mid-morning snack (*el apertivo*) might be – for a working man – a rough bread sandwich (*bocadillo*) of cheese or ham, or sardines and olives washed down with coffee, beer, water or wine. This has to last him through until 2 or 2.30pm when he will take his lunch. At mid-morning, too, in villages and towns the special snack (*tapas*) bars start to sell their unique wares – small portions of olives, squid (*calamares*), octopus (*pulpo*), anchovy (*anchoa*), mushrooms and herbs, Spanish omelette, chopped pork and parsley, and best of all *tapas variada* ('a little of each') are served hot or cold in little terracotta dishes; or as *un racion* in larger dishes, accompanied by bread, a small beer, a glass of wine or for the more reckless digestion, coffee and cognac; prices are usually very reasonable in these bars. Not only do tapas bars serve as a place to take a snack to bridge that gap from 7 or 8am in the morning until 2pm in the afternoon, they also function as a meeting-place where people can chat and talk business. Nowadays the Spanish equivalent of the 'yuppie' sits with his coffee and calculator scribbling away in his personal organiser to the clatter of plates and cups – tiled floors and marble counters make these bars noisy places.

Lunch (*la comida*, or *el almurzo*) is often the main meal of the day and can be a very protracted affair, extending to 4 or 4.30pm and including up to four or five courses (*platos*). Contrary to common belief, the Spanish do not generally drink a lot of alcohol even with their meals. Although many lunches include wine, very often you will see only a little of it being consumed as preference is given to mineral water (*agua mineral*) or lemonade (*gaseosa*).

If lunch has not been a formidable affair, a mid-afternoon snack (*la merienda*) will be taken; it is mainly favoured by mothers and children and consists of a sandwich or pastry and a drink.

Dinner (*la cena*) is usually a lighter meal than lunch and is rarely taken before 9.30 or 10pm when most larger restaurants come to life, and it can be taken as late as midnight at weekends.

Eating out is very popular in Spain, and nowadays it seems to be as fashionable to take friends out for a good meal as to entertain them at home; this may be because both partners tend to work and thus both have equal need of a break. Children are nearly always taken everywhere with the family and baby-sitting is something almost unknown, as families tend to do most things together. Children will therefore be up with the family late at night, especially during the hot summer months when the whole group will take a pre-dinner stroll (*paseo*) in the cool of the evening. Restaurants are given a rating by local government according to their standards; and an official list of prices charged (*tarrifas*) has to be submitted for official stamping before being displayed in what is often a place where the customer would find it nigh on impossible to read, for example high on the wall behind the bar. However, menus and wine lists are clearly written, and in resort areas in two or three languages; and it is never a problem finding a place to eat that suits both palate and pocket.

The set meal of the day (*menu del dia*) is usually served at lunchtime, and presents by far the best value anywhere. It includes three courses with bread and wine and rarely costs more than £3.00.

À *la carte* meals can begin with a starter (*entremeses*) of hors d'oeuvres, pasta, soup or a regional dish, followed by a fish course with vegetables (*segundo plato*); then the main course (*tercero plato*) of meat, game or sea food and rice (*paella*); and finally dessert (*postre*) – the Spanish love their desserts, and there is always a delightful range of home-made or deep-frozen sweets to choose from, with coffee and liqueurs to follow: in a modest restaurant the bill (*la cuenta*) would not exceed £10.00 per head. Tipping (*las propinas*) is a common practice in Spain and, many would claim, an essential part of the income of the person employed in the service industry. This is not necessarily true now, as the unions have established fair wage minimums for all. However, tipping is still expected and as a guide it should amount to about 10 per cent of the bill. In many bars and cheap cafeterias there is still a tin or terracotta jug (*bote*) kept for tips, and these are periodically shared out among the staff; however, sharing the tips is not a popular practice everywhere as many waiters claim that the lazy get supported by the hard workers.

Spanish customs and courtesy often cause foreigners to think that they are aloof and unnecessarily formal in their behaviour. This is far from the truth, and many Europeans could do well to take notice of the respect that Spaniards show for each other. On meeting, men shake hands – sometimes this is extended to a slight embrace if they have not seen each other for a long time, and if they are good friends or family. Women kiss each other lightly upon each cheek, and courtesy and respect are shown to both women and the elderly. This is in marked contrast to the licence young children are often allowed, running wild at formal events, though it must be said that by the age of ten or so most Spanish children are capable of amusing themselves in a more constructive way than many 'well brought up' children from other European countries.

Family events are still considered a time to push the boat out; births, marriages, first communions and scholastic presentations are all a good cause to celebrate, with a formal meal, lots of photos and now, of course, a video of the whole event. The family gathers in strength, eager to catch up on news and any events they may have missed.

Family surnames (*apellidos*) may present a bit of a mystery unless explained, and the Spanish do seem to have a lot more names than most other Europeans. Spaniards usually have two surnames, the first being the father's and the second the mother's – therefore the son of

Antonio Pujol Cortes and Maria Valasquez Vidal becomes Miguel Pujol Valasquez. When a woman marries she may be known by her maiden name, or may drop her mother's name and add her husband's as follows: Maria Ruez Talla marries Jaime Feliu Diez, and becomes Maria Ruez de Feliu; as a couple they will be known as Los Señores de Feliu. A girl will usually have Maria as one of her Christian names (*nombres*); a boy may well take his father's first name, though whilst he is young it may be reduced to the children's form – for example, Juan becomes Juanito.

Spain is going through a period of considerable social change and the traditional family unit is desperately trying to keep up. National incentive prizes used to be given to fathers who sired large families, Spain at the time being concerned to populate her vast tracts of sparsely inhabited land; the prizes (*premios*) were paid, appropriately, on Father's Day, and were to signify the male dominance or machismo which then pertained – in the last decade, however, these have disappeared. Although there is no family allowance as such paid in Spain, poor families can nevertheless submit to means testing and may then receive a small monthly allowance. Also, families with over four children (*familias numerosa*) qualify for regular support in the form of subsidised rail, boat, and plane travel on Spanish national transport; school fees are also paid or subsidised. At the present time (1990) there is a bill before government to establish a family allowance scheme similar to that in other European countries.

The Spanish at Leisure
Ask many Spaniards how they spend their free leisure time and the response will be 'What free time?'. They do work longer hours than most other Europeans; many have second jobs to augment their basic wage and (it must be said) to support their current thirst for buying all the consumer durables that are being plugged with unerring regularity on television and radio. However, putting aside their penchant for work, when they *are* free they *do* play;

31

they watch a variety of sports, and the current government policy of introducing houses of culture into most towns has encouraged a large number of people to take up a wide range of mind-improving studies from languages to cooking, and from ceramics to knitting.

The sport that appears to transcend all others in terms of its participant and watching numbers is football, closely followed by basketball (*basquet*), handball and volleyball; cycling, too, has a great following and one seldom drives along a Spanish road without seeing a gaggle pushing themselves hard in serious training. Mountain roads with 1:4 plus inclines seem to present little problem to them, nor do the hair-raising descents with hair-pin bends which follow. Golf and yachting provide entertainment and relaxation for the wealthy, and marinas spring up overnight, only to be filled with luxury yachts and motor cruisers. Shore fishing is popular, as is fishing from small boats. Most coastal families have at least one motor boat and these are well used and cared for. Octopus (*pulpo*), squid (*calamares*) and mackerel (*caballa*) are a frequent catch, and grouper and mullet are often caught around the Balearics. Swimming and tennis are popular in the summer, and now that excellent all-weather sports complexes are being built in many towns, badminton, squash, aerobics, six-a-side football, shooting and gymnastics are all getting their share of devotees.

Because of the vast tracts of wild land found in Spain it is natural that game shooting, camping, hiking and climbing should feature highly in outdoor pursuits. National parks have been established where outstanding features are found, and certain wildlife species have been protected from the ravages of the specimen gatherers – thus in some mountain regions you can still see the brown bear, the ibex and the wild sheep, plus countless species of birds and plants seldom found outside these regions. The Spanish have a great affection for caged birds and no Spanish street is without the trill of a canary or the warble of a dove. Pedigree dogs and cats are prized and well looked after, and in fact the standard of animal husbandry in Spain is higher than anywhere else in the Mediterranean. This factor would seem to be quite at odds with the national sport of bullfighting; the bullfight is said to have originated in pre-Roman times, and through various modifying influences down the centuries, it has finally been established in its present esoteric ritualistic form, followed live and on television by millions of Spaniards each summer Sunday afternoon. There is, of course, quite a vociferous anti cruel sports lobby, and they are having some effect, but to get bullfighting stopped or modified would be ten times as hard as getting the Grand National stopped in England.

Fighting bulls have been bred for hundreds of years, and the ranches which breed them have a long and complex bloodstock history, as protected as any racehorse stable. A mature fighting bull can weigh in excess of 16cwt (800kg) and in full charge can, and sometimes does, lift a horse and rider into the air – as many picadors find out. There is no space here to go into the vast ritual surrounding the bullfight, but suffice it to say that all the human participants risk their lives each time they enter the ring, even though the odds are stacked heavily in their favour. The rules of the choreography played out by the bullfighter (*torero*) contain forty to fifty passes, most of which are known by heart to the audience. All have to be executed correctly and fearlessly or the hissing and whistling will start – last season a bullfighter was physically beaten in the arena by some of the crowd for showing cowardice. Bullfighting is said to have had its origins in the north of Spain in the Navarra Pamplona region, and the running of young bulls through the streets there in July brings people from all over Europe to watch the white-clad young men chance their luck.

Turning to more restful pursuits, the Spanish do watch a lot of television. There is good coverage of news and world events; the ubiquitous soaps – *Dallas, Falconcrest, Neighbours* and *Eastenders* – have their following, as do

'Allo 'Allo, Black Adder and *Fawlty Towers* (Manuel is Italian, by the way – 'he's from Naples'). Also, as the municipal sports complexes were built, so were the houses of culture with their libraries and classrooms, and here the Spanish can attend lessons which cover a wide range of interests; these are well supported, particularly those offering foreign languages and cookery courses. Then on summer weekends, families will visit each other, or meet in the country where they will picnic under the trees. Women will often gather together in the narrow streets in the cool of the late afternoon to knit and chat whilst the children play; the men sit beneath the trees in the square (*plaza*) and yarn or play boule on a sandy strip of ground. There seems to be a more general sociability than in countries farther north, doubtless prompted to a degree by the weather. People play board games in bars, often without a drink, or with perhaps just a glass of water; and card games are also popular, though the rules may baffle the casual observer.

On the whole, the Spanish are more relaxed in their socialising; they do seem to mix more, and the further one gets from the centres of industry and commerce the more relaxed their attitude to recreational activities seems to be.

Fiestas feature regularly in the Spanish way of life; even though statistics show that regular church attendance is falling, people still celebrate with gusto their town or village saints' days. Personal saints' days are not observed so frequently; and national *fiestas*, or more accurately public holidays, are only actually celebrated by true churchgoers – the rest just take a day off work or school, whilst most shops and businesses in resort areas will ignore them altogether should they fall in the tourist season. One typically Spanish custom is known as *los puentes*: should a *fiesta* or public holiday fall on a Tuesday or Thursday, the Spanish *hacen un puente* – 'make a bridge' – and join the day off to the weekend. How sensible! They are, however, only paid for the official holiday.

One *fiesta* of note for the family falls on 1 November:

All Saints' Day (*Dia de todos los Santos*), celebrated in many parts of Spain as 'the day of the dead'. Flowers are purchased and the whole family endeavours to spend time at the cemetery, either making it a day-long vigil or just spending a little time at the graves thinking about those who have died. Some families take food and stay all day, appreciating the chance to see other relatives and have a chat. Apparently it is not particularly a sad time, just an opportunity to pay respect.

Fiestas and Holidays

Whilst the Spanish are somewhat bemused by the British preoccupation with the weather (a concern which, I might add, seems to fade after a year or two of residence in Spain), the British often wonder at the Spanish preoccupation with fiestas and saints' days. The Spanish calendar is full of saints' days and national holidays, and in a country where only 80 per cent of the population consider themselves Catholics and where (according to a recent survey) less than half of these attend mass, the foreigner is amazed to find this obsession with the observation of religious festivals.

One of the main reasons for observing them so conscientiously may be that a major fiesta means a public holiday, and banks and most public services either shut down or run a modified schedule. This, you may say, is at odds with the strong work ethic that the Spanish seem to hold; but what you must realise is that as well as enjoying work, the Spanish also have a great capacity for enjoying parties and festivals. There is a lot of dressing up and preparation in the weeks prior to the fiesta; the competition between groups and individuals to turn out in the best costumes and to design the very best floats is very keen; and dances, music and singing are all rehearsed to the smallest detail so that on the allotted day the whole event will go like clockwork, each knowing his part and throwing himself into the rôle. Beneath their apparent reserve the Spanish are a histrionic people and given the chance most will sing and dance to traditional music in an uninhibited way.

Ferias and Romerias

Every village and town in Spain has one or more patron saint or virgin whose names are usually ascribed to the various churches; each year there are fairs and pilgrimages to local shrines that are held on the day of each patron saint (*dia patrona*). Some of these fiestas have become national institutions, and even of international importance when assisted by such writers as Hemingway, and before him Cervantes. The San Fermin fiesta of Pamplona (Navarra) in northern Spain traditionally runs its young bulls through the streets (*el encierro*) in the afternoon, and this draws people from all over Europe; in part this is thanks to Hemingway's fascination with the display of *machismo* by the white-clad youths eager to impress their girlfriends and amigos with their daring – which does not extend, it must be said, to taking on the bulls in the Plaza de Toros in the evening! This is left to the highly trained *toreros* (bullfighters). There is a slightly similar fiesta in nearby Estella later in the year when women are allowed to run in the *encierro*.

With almost as much international support is the famous Fallas fiesta held during March in Valencia. Enormous papier-mâché floats are borne around the streets to the accompaniment of much music, dancing and singing. On the final day of the fiesta the grand closing ceremony consists of setting light to the floats, and letting off thousands of fireworks in one enormous frenetic display. If you plan to visit either of these major *fiestas*, book your hotel or room a long way in advance. Once after the San Fermin fiesta a guest leaving his Pamplona hotel said he would be returning the following year, which prompted the receptionist to warn him that it was best to book his room there and then – the towns do get packed for these festivals.

Other major fiestas of note include those held on

Christmas Eve, and most towns afford much more to this occasion than is usually seen in northern European areas. In Palma de Mallorca there is a curious mixture of ancient and modern in the ceremony of *Cant de la Sibilia* – 'Song of Sybil' – which forms part of the midnight mass; in the book of Sybil it is apparently prophesied that a child messiah would come.

Holy Week (Semana Santa) is celebrated everywhere, and each town and village does this in its own special way – fairs and carnivals, and processions and pilgrimages to holy shrines are all an integral part of the ceremonies. The most famous, however, take place in Seville, where great crowds of people carrying massive effigies and lighted candles parade the streets. Malaga has a similar ceremony which traditionally culminates in the release of an offender from jail; this might, one imagines, have some association with the release of Barabbas! Who knows!

New Year's Eve has a special ceremony enjoyed by Spaniards and visitors alike: some time before midnight every guest is given twelve grapes; then at each stroke of the midnight hour he must pop a grape into his mouth. A trick to help you through this rather difficult feat is to deseed your twelve grapes before you start!

Spanish children have to wait until 6 January for their presents, for according to tradition this is the day of the Three Kings (*los Reys Magos*). On Mallorca the Kings arrive by sea dressed in their royal robes, and distribute presents to the children on the shore. Plays and other ceremonies take place in other parts of Spain at this time to mark the occasion.

During the summer months fiestas are held to celebrate harvests as well as saints' days. For example, the annual wine battle in La Rioja celebrates the year's grape crop; wear old clothes if you go, as there is a lot of wine thrown around. There is also the feast of San Pedro, the patron saint of fishermen; this is celebrated with decorated fishing boats which sail around in procession, and with much merrymaking at traditional fishing ports.

The road to Santiago de Compostela in Galicia has been trodden by pilgrims since the ninth century and the story is as follows: during the reign of Alphonse II of Asturias, an old hermit said he had seen stars shining over a rocky outcrop. He told the bishop, and on investigation the body of a man in a linen shroud was discovered with symbols which made them believe it was that of Saint James the apostle. Alphonse immediately declared St James the patron saint of all Spain. The news travelled rapidly, and people set out to see this wonderful discovery. As a place of pilgrimage it soon challenged Rome, with pilgrims coming from as far away as southern Italy and northern France and establishing over the years the now famous pilgrim routes. A cathedral was built over the original site, and a city grew up around it which was called *Santiago del Campo de Estrellas* ('St James of the Field of Stars'); along the pilgrim routes appeared monasteries, convents and shelters where pilgrims could rest on their way and gather strength and pray.

The Pope made his first visit in 1982, an occasion which is thought to have revived this pilgrimage for all time. His visit in 1989 brought pilgrims from far and wide travelling on foot, donkey and even roller skates; and one hardy French girl came by windsurfer, following a blessing by her local priest.

The more conventional road routes are well documented, particularly the 250-mile (400km) way from the French border to Santiago which the priest Valino Sampedro has discussed in detail in his pilgrims' guide. This year he organised the marking of the way where it had become either overgrown or obliterated by time; thus once again it gives clear passage past old Romanesque churches and ruined forts once occupied by knights who guarded the path for travellers.

Modern-day pilgrims can win the 'Pilgrim's Diploma' by following a set route and obtaining stamps at various points. They can get free food and accommodation at some stopping places and if on arrival at Santiago their card is correctly filled in, they get their diploma and the privilege of staying free in the *Hostal de los Reyes Catolicas*. Other freelance pilgrims will find a welcome along the route with offers of food and drink and the request 'pray for me in Santiago'. This year it was estimated that more than 14,000 pilgrims travelled on foot, and the Pope's address was given to a number in excess of 300,000 – such is the revival of this ancient festival.

As the year draws on there is the Fiesta de Pilar, held in Zaragoza on 12 October, when women in their regional costume place flowers at the feet of the Virgin in the Basilica del Pilar. It is surprising to see how many Maria-Pilars there are amongst the ladies of Zarragoza, clearly demonstrating the popularity of this saint.

As well as the national saints' days, and the village and town saints' days, there are also individual saints' days (*dio mi santo*) – so if you are lucky enough to be named after a saint, you too may celebrate your own day! A warning, however: in Spain on your *dio mi santo* it is traditional to entertain your friends, so save up! Your birthday (*mi cumpleaños*) is celebrated in a similar fashion by taking your family and friends out for a meal or a drink. All Fools' Day is traditionally kept on 28 December, otherwise called Holy Innocents' Day (*el dia de los inocentes*) in remembrance of the day Herod killed all the young male children. It is celebrated in the usual manner, with harmless practical jokes being played. A favourite trick is to borrow a little money, and if the lender asks for it back, say '*que te lo paguen los santos inocentes*': 'let the holy innocents pay you back'.

All major fiestas are considered national holidays, and the most important institution to be affected are the banks which you will definitely find closed; do not, therefore, leave money-changing to a saint's day – and for ease of remembering when these are, get a Spanish calendar as they are always marked in red; besides which the calendar will help you to learn a little more of the language. Most good Spanish banks provide excellent

calendars free to their customers who ask for them; those
from the Banco Sa Nostra and the Banco Santander are
particularly attractive.

A List of Main Fiestas

Christmas Day	el dia Navidad
New Year's Day	el dia del Año Nuevo
Saint Joseph's Day	el San José (March 19)
Victory Day	el dia de Victoria (March 1)
Holy Week	Semana Santa
Good Friday	Viernes Santo
Easter	Pascua
Ascension Day	la Ascensión
Whitsun	el Pentecostés
Corpus Christi	el Corpus
Saint James	el dia de Santiago (July 25)
Assumption	la Asunción (August 15)
Virgin of Pilar/ America Day	el dia de Virgen del Pilar/el dia de la Hispanidad (October 12)
All Saints' Day	el dia de todos los Santos (November 1)
Immaculate Conception and Mother's Day	la Concepción (December 8)

3
Deciding to Go

Getting Started
If time permits, spend some time in both summer and winter in the area of your choice before committing yourself to bricks and mortar, for except on the Costa del Sol where the climate is very balanced and the population fairly consistent, regions do vary from season to season. Resorts can become ghost areas – in Ibiza, for example, almost everything closes for the winter, and in some places this can include bus services, taxis, supermarkets and butchers and even medical services. High summer can be equally unbearable with every service strained to breaking point by the influx of visitors, and water shortages and electricity cuts to name but two of the risks. Even if you are not going to a resort area, take note of the expected weather (see pp11–13); parts of Spain can be quite inhospitable in winter and the luxury of double glazing and central heating is not as widespread here as it is further north in Europe; walls are frequently only single bricked, with no cavity. All in all, if you intend to stay for a long time or indeed move here permanently, it is advisable to rent initially rather than buy. Away from the coastal strips rents are reasonable, and rented accommodation will give you a chance to find out if the area suits you and will provide a base from which to look around.

Any property you may have in the UK must be considered, too; the cost of letting it lie idle can be high, and may have to include damage from vandalism and the weather, as well as the large premiums and minimum cover demanded by the insurers to owners who leave their properties vacant for more than two months. Letting is an option, of course, but one hears dreadful stories about damage and difficult tenants even when agents have been appointed. And should you be letting a mortgaged property, the rise in the mortgage rates must also be considered. If you are contemplating a stay of over 365 days you would be well advised to know about tax liabilities and benefits affecting UK property (see pp155–6).

First or Second Residence
Assuming you are now in a position to make the move, here are a few selected guidelines which will hopefully save you time and money.

Firstly, decide if you are going to be a temporary or a permanent resident; in the case of temporary residence you may require a visa obtainable from the Spanish Consulate in London, though visas are not required by the following: those intending self employment; relatives of the self-employed; or the dependent relatives of an EC national who is already legally resident in Spain. Work permits, residence permits and extensions for long holidays or study are granted, but must be applied for locally in Spain within 90 days of your arrival. The granting of applications can be a very long-winded affair, so you are well advised to obtain some form of receipt to verify the fact that an application has been made, then if, for instance, you are involved in some traffic offence or such like, you can at least demonstrate that you have put the wheels in motion to get your extended stay legalised.

Exporting Personal Effects
For those who wish to take their household goods or a substantial volume of personal possessions with them, the procedure is somewhat complex; here it is described in a step-by-step routine.

Although many furniture removal firms carry the 'International' logo on their vans, beware! – this is no guarantee that they have ever taken a consignment to Spain where everything is different. So cast around, try the well known names and apply for their information booklet or sheet on Spain and verify the cost per cubic foot of a full or part-load. Currently this can range from £2.50 to £5.00 plus, depending on the carrier and the relative part of a load. All reputable carriers will give you a free estimate, and after the initial shock, you will probably, like many others, decide to take less than originally planned. Generally, the guiding rule should be that if the same item can be bought for up to one and a half times the UK value it is often cost-efficient to buy it in Spain and either leave your item behind, or sell it before leaving. The cost of most household items is falling in Spain (see p70) and even electrical goods like microwave ovens are now only marginally dearer when measured against the cost of getting one shipped out. Another good tip (which seems obvious but many forget to take advantage of) is to fill up everything in your consignment that would otherwise be empty – all drawers, shelf units (which won't flat pack), ovens, empty space in furniture can be filled with suitable items, thus lowering the final volume considerably. Also ensure that your transit insurance not only covers the cost of all items as new, but also takes account of replacement and transport *from the UK* – so it is wise to insure the cost of the carriers' fee as well. This may seem to be slightly over the top, but insurance rates with reputable carriers are not high, and ferries have been known to sink! Also, many carriers require payment in full before the consignment leaves the UK, so it makes sense to insure everything from the start.

Documents to be obtained in the UK
Foreign nationals who intend to establish their permanent residence in Spain are allowed to import their furniture and personal effects free of customs duty provided that the goods have been in their possession for a minimum of six months prior to their entry into Spain. However, the following will be needed:

1 Application form (*cambio de residencia*) requesting that

the head of customs allows the goods free entry into Spain. This form is obtained at the office of the Spanish Consulate General in London.

2 Two lists of all household effects, written in Spanish and stating approximate reasonable value in pesetas of each item; note should be made of the make and serial number of all electrical items, motors etc. These lists must be signed by the owner and legalised by the Spanish Consulate General in London.

3 Photocopy of the principal pages of the exporter's passport (one member of the family only) visaed by the London Spanish Consulate.

4 Owner's address in the UK, and intended address in Spain.

5 A Spanish residence permit or proof of having applied for one. Should neither be available a deposit of between 25 and 60 per cent of the total value of the goods will be required at the destination in Spain; this can be recovered on production of either a *residencia* or a work permit, together with a Certificate of First Residence from the local Spanish police. These can take up to six months to obtain, so it is advisable to get the whole procedure going before you intend moving out if possible. You have a period of up to one year in which to move your goods to Spain after the granting of the permit, so it can be done after the event if necessary.

Secondary residence

As it implies, secondary residence means a second home in Spain such as a holiday or winter home, and for this the procedure is slightly more complicated. However, the main requirements are the same as in points 1 to 4 above, though an application to the Head of Customs for a secondary residence permit (*vivienda secundaria*) should also be made. In addition, the applicant should present – both at the Spanish Consulate and at the Customs – the title deeds of his property (*escritura*) or a letting contract for a minimum period of two years. A deposit or two-year bank guarantee issued by a bank based in Spain will also be required, to ensure that any goods remain at the same property and that the property will not be sub-let by the foreign owners – it must be for the exclusive use of his family. This is intended to stop the back-door importation and selling of goods in Spain.

Taking Domestic Animals into Spain

The documents required are:

1 An export health certificate issued by a veterinary surgeon authorised by the Ministry of Agriculture in the UK, issued not more than 25 days before the animal enters Spain, stating that it is free from infection.
2 A valid anti-rabies inoculation certificate. Special arrangements will have to be with your vet for this injection as he will need at least a week's notice in order to obtain the vaccine.
3 A certificate issued by your local Ministry of Agriculture office which states that the animal has been kept in an area free from animal diseases and rabies.

None of these need to be authenticated by the Spanish Consulate General.

Professional Qualifications
If you intend to use your professional qualifications in Spain you must first get your degree, certificates and diplomas validated by the Foreign Office, whose address is: Legalisation Office, Clive House, Petty France, London SW1. Begin by taking them to a solicitor who knows you and your family – he will write a letter verifying that they are yours, and will forward them to the Foreign Office; or you may do this yourself. Currently the cost is £3.00 per document or set of documents. Once authenticated they can be produced for the purposes of obtaining a work permit in Spain. However, doctors of medicine, dentists,

psychologists and others similarly qualified may find that they have to take local examinations and/or become affiliated to similar professional bodies in Spain before they can practise (see p137 for more detailed information).

Importing Your Car

The regulations issued by the Consulate General in London are only intended as guidelines and as such are subject to change.

Current information states that British nationals who wish to change their permanent address from the UK to Spain may import their private cars into Spain free of duty, provided the car has been used and registered in their name for at least six months beforehand. It will also be exempt from Spanish VAT ((IVA) if UK VAT has been paid. However, should the amount of VAT paid be less than that levied in Spain, currently 33 per cent, the difference will need to be settled with the Spanish authorities. These exemptions are only allowed on condition that the car will not be sold or transferred within a period of one year after registration in Spain.

These are the guidelines; given below are the working facts, which are somewhat at variance with the above.

Before leaving the UK

Firstly, any person who intends to remain outside the UK for at least twelve consecutive months may apply for permission to acquire a new motor vehicle free of VAT and car tax for up to six months before the date of departure, provided it is exported within that six-month period and no later. The advantages of this scheme are indeed beneficial as they tie in nicely with the dates set out in the Spanish regulations.

Simply approach the main dealer of your chosen vehicle and he will arrange delivery of a left-hand drive car on the date you require. It must be left-hand drive because currently there is an embargo on changing UK right-hand drive cars onto Spanish plates, though how long this will last no-one knows; also, of course, the advantages of driving a left-hand drive car in Spain are self-evident. Those who have the pioneering spirit may like to go over to Belgium and purchase a tax-free car there; the routine of changing from Belgium plates to UK temporary plates is not difficult once the car is in the UK, and the cost-saving can be even greater. However, be prepared to find that your Belgium-purchased car may not quite come up to its British production specification in terms of finish and fittings. You now have a new car which you may drive in the UK for up to six months before you go, the only slight setback being that your insurance company will charge you a higher premium whilst you are in the UK because the car is left-hand drive, and you will still need a tourist's 'green card' from them for your journey to Spain, plus a bail-bond guarantee. Once you have arrived in Spain, you should observe Spanish laws on insurance (see pp89–91).

Once in Spain two factors affect the situation regarding your car, both distinctly variable. Firstly, if your stay is to be from six to eight months or less you may keep and use your car on its UK plates, provided you do not engage in any work or business in Spain during that period. You should drive on an international driving licence, or have a translation made of your UK licence legalised by the UK Spanish Consulate before leaving. In Spain, all these documents must be kept in your car at all times, together with your DVLC ownership documents and insurance – photocopies are not acceptable.

If you are going to work in Spain, or retire there, you will be getting a resident's permit (*residencia*): holders of work permits and *residencia* may only drive cars on Spanish plates, and in this case you will have to exchange your UK driving licence for a Spanish one by taking it along to the local traffic police office. You are also advised to apply to the DVLC for a duplicate UK licence before parting with your own, or at least to make a photocopy of it, to substantiate a re-application for a UK licence should this be needed at some future date. Your UK plated car will also have to be changed on to Spanish plates, and for this procedure you will need the assistance of a solicitor (*gestor*) who will deal with the police department (*traffico*) and the MOT (*industria*). Both will vet your car and its documents, and you will have to pay a registration fee plus the *gestor*'s fee. You will also have to contact an importing agency who will require certain details in order that you may pay the balance of your IVA. You may have avoided VAT payment altogether in the UK by buying tax free, in which case you will have to pay 33 per cent of the car's value, less a discount for the time you have owned it.

If the car was VAT paid in the UK you will only be required to pay a proportion of the difference between UK VAT and Spanish IVA, depending again on the period you have owned the car.

In addition to the DVLC ownership document, if you intend to import you will need the original bill of sale showing whether or not VAT was paid. You will also require a Certificate of First Residence which can be applied for at your police headquarters at the time you apply for your *residencia*. During the time your *residencia* or work permit is being processed you may drive on UK plates unchallenged, but do not drive a UK-plated car once your *residencia* is through or the car may well be confiscated and sold – it does happen, so be warned!

The alternatives are either long-term contract hire (see p165), or purchasing a car in Spain (which can be problematical). Once again, UK residents fall into two categories: those intending to work, to carry on a business, or to retire permanently; and those who will be going back to the UK at intervals not longer than from six to eight months apart. So let's deal with the latter first.

We have already seen that these 'short-term' residents can keep their UK car on UK plates; however, as a temporary resident you can also purchase a car free of taxes from any Spanish dealership and have it registered on Spanish tourist plates. You will be required to state that you are not staying in Spain for more than six to eight months in any calendar year, and are not engaging in any work or business activity. The routine for obtaining a tourist-plated car does vary from region to region, but as a general guideline the dealer's *gestor* will require your passport details, your driving licence, and a copy of the deeds of your residence or a copy of the contract if you are renting. Once registered, only you or your family may drive the car and the plates will have to be renewed after twelve months when another payment will have to be made.

If at some time you apply for work or a *residencia* you may convert your tourist-plated car to a regular Spanish-plated car upon payment of the balance of IVA, which will be reduced depending on the time you have owned the vehicle. For instance, if you have had the car for four or five years the residual balance of IVA to pay will be minimal.

Another tip if you are returning to the UK at intervals for more than one month as stated above: you may only legally drive a tourist-plated car in Spain for six to eight months in the year, so in order not to lose that usage time whilst you are out of Spain you can get the customs authorities to seal your car when you leave, and the tourist period will recommence only when they break the seals on your return. Your dealer or *gestor* will advise you on the procedure for this.

Car ownership is therefore not the simple matter it is in the UK, because if you intend working you must drive on Spanish plates with a Spanish driving licence. You may buy a new or second-hand Spanish-plated car and get it legalised into your name, but you must produce your *residencia* or work permit, your deeds or a property rental contract valid for at least six months, and your passport. Once on Spanish plates you will have to pay car insurance, and road fund which is about £20.00 a year. The first MOT is due at ten years.

Vehicle insurance
Car insurance is a lot more expensive in Spain than in the UK. The bottom-of-the-range car can cost £200 per

annum to insure third party only, even before no claims discount; however, on production of a no claims bonus certificate from your UK insurers you will be allowed up to 50 per cent discount, though not the 60 per cent allowed by some UK insurers. Several UK insurance firms operate through Spanish franchises, and you would be well advised to insure with one of these even though they may charge marginally more for their services than the Spanish firms. Very few people take out fully comprehensive insurance because of the prohibitive cost, so third party fire and theft seems to be the general cover. Should you have the misfortune to become involved in an accident do not attempt to move the car until the police have been informed; they will be judge and jury, and all you have to do is to exchange insurance details with the other driver – in these circumstances you will find your English-speaking insurance representative a boon.

A word on parking in Spain: the restrictions are everywhere strongly enforced, with tow-away vehicles and clamps becoming very popular ways of deterring offenders. International 'No Parking' signs clearly show zones, and in most towns there are ample pay-and-stay car parks. You will also find the unique ORA system, where you purchase parking tickets in bulk from a *tabacalaria* (tobacco shop) – when a ticket is required, you punch holes in the date and time with a biro yourself and display it in your car window; this system is now catching on in big cities, so look for the ORA ZONA signs and go to a tobacco shop for some 1½, 1 and ½ hour tickets – they are a bright innovation for a problem and only cost 75, 50 and 25 pesetas respectively.

If you feel that car ownership is too much of a bother, a viable and cheap means of personal transport in this equable climate is the humble moped or scooter, which although a bit more expensive to purchase in Spain than in the UK, does provide a means of getting from A to B for very little running cost.

A word on petrol
Petrol prices are government-controlled, and are currently below those charged in the UK. NORMAL is 92 octane, SUPER is about 97 octane, MEZCLA is a 25:1 mixture for 2-stroke engines, and GASOIL is diesel. Many petrol stations have bars and restaurants which a British visitor may find surprising after experiencing the tough UK drink-and-drive laws; but petrol stations are often the only break on vast stretches of road, so they serve as service areas as well as to dispense fuel. In every town in Spain there is usually a rota of petrol stations open all night; on fiestas, look in the local papers and keep your tank at least half full at all times. Many residents carry a spare can in the back of their vehicle.

Drinking and driving
A driver is usually only breathalised if he is involved in an accident, and the legal limits are similar to those set out in the UK. Currently there is a bill before the European Parliament to bring all EC members into line on drinking and driving laws, though it would be difficult to imagine Spain conforming to this unless there is a total change in her way of life; for whilst it is true that one does witness horrendous accidents, especially at night when people have been drinking, there does not seem to be the same outrage as in the UK press. Nor does Spain experience such appalling weather conditions which can tend to exacerbate accidents and cause multiple pile-ups on the motorways. Furthermore, there are far fewer vehicles per road mile. So, with vast tracts of country to be explored and with easier driving conditions altogether, Spain is indeed a pleasant place in which to motor.

Moving Out
Personal effects
If you are taking furniture and personal effects you will by now have visited the Spanish Consulate with all your documents and engaged the services of an international

removal firm. They will have sent you a pack containing an estimate for the move, an insurance proposal form and a schedule of the documents they will require to get your effects into Spain. Presumably you will also have an address in Spain with either the deeds in your possession if the property is yours, or a long-term contract for a let of not less than six months.

The removal firm will, if asked, deliver in advance containers which you pack yourself beforehand; however, it is not usual for them to insure the contents of these containers against breakages in transit, for the fairly obvious reason that they need to see their condition before packing.

You will also have contacted your vet and the Ministry of Agriculture and Fisheries if you are taking pets; and if you are not transporting them with you, the services of a specialist animal carrier will have been sought.

The UK tax authorities and the DHSS will have sent you their documents, which you are well advised to complete and get checked before leaving the UK; and your bank will have been advised of your change of address.

Getting There

When all these things have been done, it is time to go: for most people, this is a time of mixed excitement and sadness when clear thinking becomes a little impaired, so it really is advisable to keep check-lists blue-tacked to some convenient spot so you can tick things off as you go.

If you are going by car, and particularly if you are taking pets, use the Plymouth/Santander Brittany Ferries route. The cost may seem a little high, but the saving in time and sheer convenience makes up for it, especially if you are travelling to southern Spain or the Balearics. Your animals will only have to go through one border control, and Santander is very efficient in this respect with a health official usually available at the dock.

Understandably, you may be considering taking expensive and fragile items in the car with you. However, you should be warned that customs clearance in Spain is very complex and best left to the experienced carriers – rarely, if ever, do things get broken, so let them do the job and save yourself time and worry. Also bear in mind that a full car with a roof-rack is a very vulnerable target for thieves should you have to leave it unattended at any time. If you have to overnight in an hotel, unload everything; it's a bind, but well worth while (for crime in Spain, see pp106–10).

The Arrival of Your Effects

Your removal firm will have given you the name and address of their agent in Spain, and you should contact him as soon as you arrive as he will require certain documents from you in order to clear customs. If you are taking up permanent residence you will not be directly liable to import taxes if all items are over six months old, as long as you have receipts for anything that might cause doubt; however, charges will be made for customs clearance, and the agent will also demand his fee. Also there is a matter of a deposit being required until your final residence permit has been granted: this is currently between 40 and 60 per cent of the total declared value of the goods on mainland Spain, and 25 per cent of their declared value if you are importing them onto the Balearics. So if you are taking a large quantity of effects with you, do budget for this – and don't expect to see the money back for a while. Your Spanish bank can put up a bond for you if they are given sufficient warning, the advantage being that you do not have to change valuable sterling into pesetas unnecessarily. It goes without saying, of course, that you cannot earn interest on this amount whilst the bank is giving guarantee. To get your effects released from customs the agent will require photocopies of your passport, copies of your deeds or letting contract and a certificate from the British Consul in your area to say that you have until now been a resident in the UK and that this is your 'first' residence in Spain.

A few points worth remembering when your effects

arrive: should you live somewhere where the removal vehicle cannot reasonably reach, such as a narrow un-made road, you may be charged for a shuttle service by some local carrier; and similarly, if you live in a particularly awkward apartment where furniture has to be hoisted through windows or the terrace this will also collect a further charge. Be quite sure, therefore, that the carriers know what they are facing before they leave the UK, and then a fixed price can be worked out for the job; it is difficult to negotiate sensibly when your furniture is standing half a mile away and their time is money. Check everything as soon as it arrives – whilst the carrier is still there, if possible, so any breakages can be filed with the agent immediately and an express copy sent to the insurers.

There are no quarantine regulations for pets in Spain, so provided all their documents are in order you will be able to collect them from the airport without any problem should you have left their transit in the hands of an agent. Most domestic animals settle very readily once they have surveyed their territory and even the furriest, fluffiest of cats seems to survive the blistering heat by finding a cool corner on a tiled floor. So long as animals have plenty of fresh water available, and are introduced to their change of diet slowly, they will adapt. Anyway, animal products such as Pal, Chum, Whiskas, and Kit-e-Kat are available (at a price), although fresh products are much cheaper, with small fish at 20 pence a kilo, and offal and bones at about a £1.00 a kilo – so that on the whole, animals are better fed.

Depending on the season you arrive, about half your wardrobe will need to be stored away; most people use cabin trunks or chests, with liberal quantities of mothballs. Do watch the humidity, however, as clothes hung in a wardrobe for long periods do grow some interesting flora if not watched. One answer to this problem is to place a low wattage bulb on the floor of the wardrobe – the slight warming and air circulation seem to do the trick. Other people just move everything out periodically and hang it in the sun with equally good results.

4
A Place to Live

Long or Permanent Stays

At the last government count it was estimated that there were about 1.5 million foreign property owners in Spain; add to that an estimated 55 million foreign tourists each year, and taking Spain's population of only 38 millions, there are times when foreigners almost equal or out-number the indigenous people. It is therefore reasonable to imagine that Spain is well geared up to dealing with foreigners buying or renting property, and in fact it is. For Spaniard and foreigner the procedures are identical, and once contracts have been signed you as foreigner have equal rights concerning ownership or tenure. This leaves you with just the choice of accommodation that you require, and that will of course be determined to some degree by your proposed length of stay.

Many hostels, pensions, small hotels and guest houses will undertake very favourable long term contract rates if approached out of season. Whilst the holiday season is booming, Spanish single-mindedness prevails and it is difficult to get many of them to talk objectively about the off-season period, but approached in late October or early November their long stay half-board terms will surprise you. Many people – generally the old colonial – who have been used to living in an hotel as a way of life, choose to spend their declining years in some of Spain's older establishments; these offer suites as well as rooms, tiny kitchenettes with fitted fridges and cookers where simple meals can be prepared – so if you are inclined to that way of life, the option is there.

Certainly renting offers the best and safest initial choice; flats and studios away from the sacred front line can be rented on long or short term contract, and they do give you an opportunity to find out if the area really suits you. The resort that was alive and fun to live in in the summer months may suddenly die in late October, with all but a few essential services closing and most of the residents leaving for their permanent homes; you could therefore find yourself marooned in a deserted town with the prospect of having to travel many miles, on a reduced public transport schedule if you have no car, to buy your essentials. Renting also gives you some idea of the size and type of accommodation you require. Many settlers already own small studios and one-bedroom flats which are ideal for the summer and which they have used for years prior to coming out on a long stay; but they find out all too soon that these are far from adequate for year-round living – nowhere to put those bits and bobs so essential to life, and wardrobe and drawer space geared to the storage of only lightweight summer clothing. Parts of Spain get very cold in the winter – some colder than in the UK – and summer flats are not heated; also, butane fires cause fumes that some people cannot tolerate. For all-year-round living, an apartment with a fire-place in which to burn logs, or one which is centrally heated, is therefore really the best bet.

These are some of the points in favour of renting initially whilst you look around, and in the long term you may consider the advantages of renting permanently. If you can sell your property in the UK at a favourable price, that money invested wisely in offshore funds will provide a very handsome return which should more than cover the rental of even an expensive property, and still leave enough to live on comfortably, plus a little for capital appreciation. Admittedly, because of the hiccups in housing prices over the past two decades, British people are reticent to leave the housing market for fear of never being able to buy back in at a reasonable standard, and they are wise to maintain this stance if they live in the UK or intend moving back. However, property prices in Spain are not so erratic, and many people choose not to break into their capital to buy property, particularly if they are of advanced years and wish to leave their money to their families in the UK – laws of inheritance in Spain are complex and full of problems (see pp160–1). Whichever you do, it is swings and roundabouts; property prices in Spain have steadily increased over the past ten years, and a property bought in 1978 is now (1990) worth roughly double what you paid for it. However, as in the UK, the property market has levelled out, particularly as people wait to see what 1992 will bring.

Whether renting or buying, your choice will be governed by much the same criteria: area, position, proximity, cost, accessibility and amenities to hand. Nationality zones can be found in all the popular resort areas, and they are now becoming established inland, too, as conservationist pressure on coastal development forces builders and people further away from the coast. Which nationality dominates can be found out simply by reading the café menu boards – the dishes offered and the languages used will soon tell you who is being catered for. For the rather timid new settler it is often reasurring to be surrounded by your own nationality, people who will advise you when you encounter problems; and in some of the national strongholds the local administration will even circulate information sheets in the dominant foreign language, advising when, for example, the local rates and taxes have to be paid – some even send a circular showing how your rate money is being spent. So the message is: if you like being amongst your own nationality, and if you never intend taking the Spanish language further than being able to order a coffee or a beer, then the mini-Englands are for you.

Which way a property faces is of great importance in Spain; north-facing blocks of flats will suffer the full onslaught of cold winter winds unrelieved by sunny hours, so take your compass with you when you go hunting – the sun doesn't shine all day, every day, and agents have been known to suffer extreme disorientation when a likely sale or let is in prospect. If you are considering a block of flats, go back after the agent has dropped you off and try to talk to a resident; ask about *any* problems that might be relevant – drainage, lifts, redecoration programme, new wiring due, swimming-pool filtration due for replacement; *you* will be paying for these if you buy, and many rental contracts, too, leave you responsible for the community charges.

The proximity of the property to other amenities can be both a blessing and a bane; being near the shops and the beach and having a pleasant view over the bay or harbour is most agreeable, but this does have its setbacks: it is often a lively area at night, with music bars, discos and an accompanying volume of people and traffic on the street until all hours of the night during the season. True, the higher you go the more you see and the less you hear – but don't expect tranquillity *anywhere* on the coast, for whilst Spain passes laws to restrict the playing of music that can be heard from the street after midnight, she cannot legislate to control street noise, and this is often much louder than the music.

Moving slightly away from the coastal strip has many advantages if you choose carefully. Hill properties often command attractive views, and local shops can readily meet your day-to-day needs. Do, however, make sure that the shops are open all year, or you may find that after the end of October you have a long trek for your bread and milk.

The Rental Contract
Rental contracts are usually drawn up by Spanish solicitors or qualified estate agents. They are legally binding by both parties, and should contain the following information:

1 Period of contract.
2 Monthly rental showing the proportion charged for the property, and the proportion charged for furniture and fittings.
3 Any payment or charges the tenant is liable for – for

example: electricity, telephone, rates, community charges.
4 Insurance liability.
5 Rights for renewal.
6 Responsibility for repairs.

For your part, you may be asked to pay a refundable deposit against damages and also to pay a stipulated amount of money in advance. In the case of an expensive property you will almost certainly be asked to produce references, and your bank manager may help you with this. The great advantage of sensible renting is that it does leave the tenant freedom of movement between properties without the penalties of sale costs. He can change the style and size of his home to suit his needs, and if the whim takes him he can pack up and move back to the UK or elsewhere at short notice. His capital is intact, and his kith and kin are safe to inherit his wealth should he die.

On the minus side, he will be hard pressed to find a rented property that will really feel like home. Other people's taste in furniture and fittings is something he will have to live with, and alterations cannot be made in this respect. All in all, buying a property is really the only solution for those intending a very long stay, or who in fact plan to reside permanently in Spain.

Buying a Property in Spain

There are two things which are of paramount importance when you consider property purchase in Spain: first, the help of a good English-speaking estate agent (*inmobiliaria*); and second, the services of an established solicitor who either speaks English or has a secretary who does.

Buying a property is a minefield, and you are wise to rent first and look around only when you have tested the water.

Estate agents keep lists of properties on their books, as do UK agents; however, unlike the UK, they also keep a careful eye on all new developments and local happenings and are able to negotiate prices with any seller or developer whether the property is on their books or not. They are also – like their UK brethren – capable of extensive poetic licence when it comes to description. The 'elevated and quaint rustic property with extensive views situated amid olive terraces within easy walking distance of shops and with the possibility of electricity and water being laid on' may be an olive farmer's storage shed half-way up a mountain side, with no chance whatsoever of permission being given for any form of occupancy since the area is designated by law as rural land (*rustica*), for agricultural use only.

Do not, however, lose heart: there are scores of properties for you to see, especially if you have a reasonable sum to spend. A current guide (which would include payment of all the fees mentioned later) would be as follows:

£9,000–£20,000:	Studio or 1-bedroom flat in coastal resort depending on line;
£15,000–£75,000+:	1, 2, 3-bedroom, 2-bathroom apartment as above;
£60,000–£180,000:	2, 3, 4-bedroom, 2-bathroom house in urbanisation development or penthouse flat;
£100,000–£200,000:	Detached country house in own grounds in varying stages of modernisation – pool, garages, buildings, trees, etc – or super luxury flat;
£100,000+ :	Rustic farm with grounds and houses.

These prices are only intended as a rough guide and will vary greatly from one resort to another, and from region to region. Furthermore, inland village houses with patios and small gardens are currently selling for £5,000, if you can adapt to a totally Spanish way of life; however, please don't think that for one moment the locals will greet you will open arms, because many of these places have changed little since Franco's time and there is still a reticence about accepting anything that is different. Regional dialects and even language itself may mean difficulties in communication at even the most basic level, so do take care – think twice before you fly off and go native.

Also to be considered are the factors which governed the original building of your intended purchase. Many houses were – and are still being – built without permission, on land designated as non-urban land; in a recent case whole blocks of flats and holiday homes were bulldozed to the ground because they had been constructed in a 'green belt' area of the coast (*zona verde*). Had this happened in England the owners would at least have registered some form of protest, or been present at the demolition; but in Spain they knew they were wrong from the start, chose to take a chance, and philosophically accepted the consequences – in the Spanish, *que sera, sera*. By the same token, however, they would have sold those properties to some unwitting buyer – many were seen on the market immediately before the government move – so tread carefully, and make sure you are buying a legally constructed property.

In all these cases your estate agent should be able to advise you, for unlike Britain where almost anyone can set up a property-selling business, Spain has now started to crack down on all estate agencies: prospective operators are required to be conversant with all aspects of property development and management, and to belong to the Society of Estate Agents, a regulatory body who will vet all applicants before they can join. So help is on the way, albeit slowly, and the advice is: if your agent is not an affiliated member of the society, change to one who is – there are enough of them about.

Having established that your property is legally built, what happens next? First, a word on deposits: in Spain, deposits are not normally returnable, for whatever the reason; it is therefore up to your agent or solicitor to be quite sure that the sale will go through before you part with any money. With an already constructed property this will usually be safeguarded by depositing the deeds (*escritura*) with some third party, perhaps the *notario* who will legalise the sale; he will hold them, and the deposit, until the sale goes through.

Property debts
Your agent or solicitor must then confirm that there are no debts on the property, as all debts in Spain pass with the deeds to the buyer. Gas and electricity bills, rates and telephone, builders, water, refuse collection and septic tank emptying can all be left unpaid for long periods in Spain, and can amount to many thousands of pounds when totted up. Most important of all is the debt outstanding from a mortgage, and here it is best to illustrate the problem with an actual recent case.

Where a mortgage is granted by a bank, two deeds are made out: one for the value owned by the buyer, and one for the value advanced by the bank. In this particular case, both deeds were presented at the notary at the time of signing for the purchase, the vendor was paid the money to settle the mortgage, and one full deed was made out for the property – but the vendor then failed to settle the mortgage. The bank then claimed that amount from the new owner. So the golden rule is always that if there is an outstanding mortgage, get your agent or solicitor to settle it from the sale money before paying any balance to the vendor. Also, be sure to obtain clearance-of-debt receipts from all services used by the vendor on that property; this sounds difficult, but may turn out to be quite simple as once the vendor realises your agent is on his trail he will probably go round and settle all his debts anyway, so that the sale can go ahead unhindered.

Building Your Own Home
Already under construction
Question one: is the property being built legally? And question two: will it ever be finished? If you have been visiting Spain for a number of years you will doubtless have

seen, time after time, various half-completed blocks at some stage of construction. The stories are legion, but the three reasons are usually illegal building, funds suddenly running out, and finally (and by no means uncommon) the constructor dying and a monumental probate argument ensuing between his beneficiaries.

A reasonably safe rule is this: buy only when the building is completed, or at least at the stage where people are actually occupying part of the development; for then at least you know you will have allies who have fully paid and who will be in a strong legal position should anything go amiss.

A further consideration is change of use: recently, a very attractive development was being constructed with the proposal of 2,000 villas, a swimming complex, tennis courts, shops and other services. Forty houses had been built, when the local government announced that the whole area was being re-designated as a marina and holiday complex. The poor builder was given his money back, but although the occupiers of the forty houses have been told they are safe, the total change of their future environment has gone unconsidered. This story, however, does have a happy ending, for if all goes well and the marina is built, the value of the properties will increase five-fold overnight; so no-one is grumbling yet!

The site
Set back from resort areas, building land is cheap though of course it will vary depending upon accessibility; for instance, on a rocky mountain side it will be very expensive to develop as roads will have to be cut and the site levelled. Also the availability of services – water, electricity and telephone – will determine the cost of the site. Mountain sites of three or more acres without facilities can be bought for as little as £5,000, whereas level urban sites can fetch upwards of £40,000 depending on the location; so you can see there is a massive discrepancy in the price of a site, although this may well level out when the property is

completed if they are both to enjoy the same facilities.

Only buy a site through a recognised agency, and ensure that you have the building permission *in writing* before you part with a single *peseta*. Carefully check the size of the development allowed; it will be in square metres and cannot be exceeded, so if your dream villa does not conform to those dimensions – keep looking around.

The building
The building cost can be roughly estimated in square metres of construction and will range between £150 and £300 depending on the standard of structure and the difficulty of preparing the site. This price will not include the architect's plans and fees, and the cost of presenting these plans to the College of Architects, which must be done before a municipal building licence is granted. In a recent case, someone received an estimate for £60,000 for the site purchase and construction, but ended up paying nearly double that amount. This was prompted by two factors – he wanted some last-minute changes made; and during the course of construction, the value of the pound dropped markedly against the *peseta*, leaving him with a lot of money to find. There is a great temptation to leave money in sterling whilst building is being carried out in the hope that the pound will gain and make the cost cheaper. However, the reverse can also happen, so change the full cost into *pesetas* at the time of signing – you can still get *some* interest on a *peseta* deposit account.

Purchase procedure
Firstly, a word or two on giving power of attorney (*poderes generales*), the power to sign in your stead. An English estate agent working in Spain was heard to say that he was horrified to see the blasé way in which prospective property purchasers signed away the access to thousands of pounds of their money to a person they had only known briefly. In the UK they would never act in such a way unless their solicitor was involved, and even then they would insist

on reading all the documents. No-one can give a logical explanation for this phenomenon, except to say that it goes on almost daily in Spain. The agent went on to say that currently, he had access to nearly half a million pounds in various clients' accounts; he was honest, but many had absconded with less. The moral is: don't ever sign away your power of attorney unless it is quite impossible for you to be on the spot when your signature is needed, and if as a result, the deal is likely to fall through. If you must give power of attorney to anyone, grant it to a reliable person well known to you, or better still to your solicitor in Spain – he dare not misuse it, or his living would be lost.

Now, back to business: assuming that the validity of the sale has been confirmed and the deeds have been produced and checked, you will then be expected to produce the funds for the purchase. An initial purchase will probably mean conversion of sterling into pesetas, so use your 'convertible peseta account' to exchange the money (there are advantages, see p153). If you have the whole sum you will visit the *notario* (justice) together with the vendor and a new deed will be sworn in your name. If you are happily married you are strongly advised to record the deed in your joint names, then on the demise of either partner the other automatically inherits without the need for probate being given. You should ask for a photocopy of the new deed of the property (*escritura de compraventa*) as the original will have to go on a long trail of offices and government departments before you finally receive it back covered in rubber stamps and signatures.

Do not think that this is the end of paying. Established properties attract an added value tax, literally: it is called *plus valia* and whilst the vendor is responsible for its payment you may, in some autonomous regions, be made to pay a small contribution. However, by far the biggest taxes to be paid are the property transfer taxes. First, IVA which is similar to British VAT – the amount paid varies on the circumstances of the sale, eg new property, old property, converted property etc, and currently ranges from 6 to 12 per cent. To circumvent paying this tax on the whole cost of the transaction, the deeds will show a 'declared' figure – a figure that the tax office is likely to accept as a reasonable price for the property. It is upon this figure that the IVA and the *plus valia* will be calculated. No-one nowadays tries to be too clever by quoting a greatly reduced figure; in times past, only about one-tenth of the value was declared – now it is more likely to be nearer two-thirds of the selling price. Finally, your agent's and/or solicitor's fees will probably come to 1 or 2 per cent of the price – not cheap, but remember that in Spain, only the purchaser pays the bills; the vendor gets off scot-free, except for *plus valia* if this is levied.

The procedure for obtaining a mortgage from your bank is similar to that adopted in the UK and requires no further explanation except to say that the bank holds its deeds and you hold yours.

From the moment of leaving the notary's office you are responsible for all your property's debts, so be sure that you inform the following services that you are the new owner and get the appropriate direct debit mandates to your bank so that payments are made on time; in Spain, penalties swiftly follow unpaid bills:

1 Local municipal authority – council offices.
2 Electricity company (GESA or the like).
3 Community owners if you are on an estate or in a block of flats.
4 Telefonica (telephone company).
5 Butano – this is the company that supplies bottled gas and most properties have at least one appliance. In each case a new contract will be made out in your name, and in the case of Butano a deposit may be required.

It sounds a lot, and believe me there's much more to it, but at least it gives you a good guide as to what is happening. Where you are not sure, ask for English translations – they will charge for them, but you will at least know what you are signing.

Water, Water, Everywhere!
Because of Spain's geographical position and the prevailing climatic conditions, it is obvious that in certain areas of seasonal high occupancy water shortages are bound to occur. Thus you may turn on a tap and without warning just a hiss of air comes out; this may go on for only a few days, or for much longer at a busy time in resort areas. So, what can be done to alleviate the problem? Modern houses and blocks of flats have large water depositories built into them – a three-bedroomed house will have a reserve large enough to keep a family of four going for at least a week, and with sensible conservation for even longer. If the house you are buying hasn't got a water deposit or a well, you would do well to consider having one built. Roof-mounted tanks can be made to look quite attractive with a terracotta tile finish. Underground tanks are cheaper to build and can be of whatever size you like; you will, however, have to purchase an electric pump to get a decent pressure throughout the house. Currently water pumps cost around £300; running costs are negligible. Many houses built on hillsides and many flats on upper floors have pumps installed at construction, so don't be surprised if you hear a high pitched whine when you turn on the tap.

Most water in mid- and southern Spain has a hefty deposit of lime in solution; this makes washing difficult and leaves a deposit on all water-heating pipes and appliances. Water softeners can be added to washing water and bath water but still the kettle, water heater and washing machine suffer. The only real answer is to install a water softening unit and to change the filter system regularly, though it is doubtful if this is really cost-effective, and it is not really worthwhile except in a new property where there has not been any furring already. The Spanish name for lime deposit is *cal*, and washing powders and dish-washer detergents are now being marketed under such names as Calgon; these are certainly effective in new appliances, but are quite disastrous in old ones as they break up the lime deposits which then block up the piping even faster.

All over the hotter parts of Spain you will see big tankers with the words AGUA POTABLE on their side and a telephone number. This is the answer for most people; the tanker arrives, pumps water into your depository and you are charged for the volume of water per litre, plus a charge for the distance it has been hauled. If you choose to live in the hills or out in the sticks it will almost certainly be the only way to get your water. Currently a tanker-full hauled out about 6 miles (10km) will cost about £25.00 for 12,000 litres and should last you a month or two; one big advantage is that it is good enough to drink from the tap, and the lime content will be much lower than in the town supplies.

Having dealt with water coming into the house, let's now look at it as it leaves. If you are lucky enough to be on mains drainage you should have little problem, except perhaps at times of torrential rainfall when manhole covers tend to become dislodged; you will pay a charge for your drainage which is a part of your annual rates (*contribucion*) payment. However, many properties are not fortunate enough to be connected to the mains sewers, and it is in this instance that the septic tank, or *pozo* as it is called, finds its way onto your property. Septic tanks seem to work well in the UK – the solid material degrades away and the liquid filters off into the ground without causing a problem. In Spain where a lot of properties are built straight on to bedrock a problem occurs: where does the water go? The answer, of course, is that it doesn't go anywhere; you have to pay to have your tank pumped out periodically by a contractor who will charge about £40.00 for the unpleasant task. If your builder has been unwise enough to route the rainwater drainage into your septic tank you will have to pay quite frequently in the rainy season to have it drained; so check, make sure the roof and path water go off elsewhere as this alone can save you a lot of money.

Many septic tanks in resort areas are so inadequate that they cause major problems in the summer once all the flats are full and showers are working non-stop; so once again, take care when you buy – ask around, and in the summer, sniff around!

5
Day-to-day Living

Shopping
With increased affluence pertaining in Spain, consumer spending has kept pace with wages and everywhere, on bill boards and on television commercials, one is encouraged to buy. The result of this campaign by the producers has been a massive increase in the number of retail outlets, from small village-type shops (*tiendas*) to giant out-of-town hypermarkets (*hipermercados*). The spin-off from all this has been a sharp increase in competition, and everywhere one is assailed by posters showing special offers (*ofertas*) – in many cases used as loss leaders to seduce the customer into the store; but rest assured, for every discount there is a commensurate increase in price somewhere on the shelves, so shop around.

Most towns have a market which is purpose-built with permanent stalls; those places too small to support a fixed market may well have a weekly street market, and here one will find equally good buys. Markets thrive in Spain and the prices and quality of produce is amazing; so, too, is the way the stall-holders display their produce, the precarious pyramids of fruit, nuts, vegetables and other fare all immaculately clean and very attractive to the customer.

Over the past ten years there has been very little, if any change in the price of most fruit and vegetables, with the exception of seasonal variations; beautiful oranges can still be bought for 25 pence a kilogram, giant lettuce for the same price. Peppers and artichokes, cucumber, melons and grapes, onions and garlic, carrots and spinach – all these have remained stable in price; only the famous green beans and cultivated mushrooms seem to have increased in price. Certainly a family of four would not spend much more than £7.00 a week on fruit and vegetables, and this is allowing for the fact that in Spain there is a tendency to eat a more vegetarian diet anyway, especially in the heat of high summer. Naturally the keeping quality of all fruit and vegetables is good due to its freshness, but nevertheless many people do shop daily either for the fun of it or because of the social contact it provides – small groups of Spanish women can often be seen chatting together near the market stalls; their complaints about quality and prices mystify the foreigner who is used to paying much more for lower quality produce.

A visit to the butcher's stall (*carneceria*) or the fish stall (*pescaderia*) will now bring you back to reality, but do not lose heart – wise and selective buying can still produce a shopping bill lower than anywhere else in Europe. If you crave English-type steaks such as fillet, expect to pay £5.00 a pound; stewing beef is about £1.50 a pound and liver the same price. Lamb is costly, too, at £2.50 a pound for leg and £3.50 for chops. Pork on the other hand is excellent value; the meat is always trimmed of all fat before weighing and you should expect to pay about £1.60 a pound for boned leg, £2.00 a pound for loin, £3.00 for fillet and £1.50 a pound for chops; the quality of this meat is excellent, and next to chicken, currently provides the best buy available. Spare ribs for barbecuing can cost as little as 70 pence a pound, and they are very meaty.

Poultry and game prices do vary according to the season, but at no time should fresh corn-fed chicken cost much above 50-70 pence a pound. Whole breast fillets cost £2.00 a pound or less, and drumsticks and wings from around 70 pence a pound. Turkey is slightly dearer, as is duck and rabbit, but they are all fresh – if a bargain price is found they can be popped into the freezer for later use.

Fish, however, is very costly, and it is worthwhile looking at the reason for this before we consider prices.

How many more fish in the sea?
The traditional idea of the picturesque fishing village
with its terracotta roofed houses and brightly coloured
boats bobbing in an azure bay is disappearing as fast as
the fish that were once caught. Whilst no good restaurant menu is complete without its fish dishes, the price
charged nowadays will make the average customer wince
– so why the massive all-round increase in price? Perhaps
a look back at the unbridled exploitation of past decades
may well provide some of the answers. For centuries past
men have cast their nets into the Mediterranean, and
have hauled in and eaten everything they have caught;
with the advent of pale blue micro net material they still
fished for everything, no matter how small the size – they
caught more and they caught smaller, and now there is
precious little left.

Spanish fishing boats are having to go further and further afield to fill their holds. Recent disputes with British
and Icelandic fisheries indicate this need to extend their
hunting grounds; Spanish deep-sea trawlers now go as far
as the Nova Scotia Grand Banks to fish for the cod and
hake so highly prized by the restaurateur. To balance this
dearth of fish we do, however, see a good sustained level
of the mollusc and polyp populations around Spain, and
there is a whole range of shellfish, from the exotic oyster
to the lowly winkle, which seems to be inexhaustible and
provides appetising fare to those settlers willing to try
something new.

Those are some of the reasons: now for some of the
prices. Small hake £3.00 a pound, large hake and cod
£3.70 a pound, sole £5.50 a pound, Red Sea bream £2.50
a pound, swordfish £6.00 a pound; but mackerel 50 pence
a pound. Trout £1.50 a pound, octopus 70 pence a pound,
squid £2.00 a pound, sardines 50 pence a pound and tur-
bot £5.00 a pound. There are, of course, slight seasonal
variations but these are no more than 25 per cent either
way. These prices are for fresh fish; frozen fish prices are
often less than half those shown above.

British brands of frozen fish are finding their way into the Spanish supermarket cold cabinets, but the prices are quite high by comparison with their Spanish counterparts.

Hypermarkets
Nowhere will you find a greater variety of goods for sale than in a Spanish hypermarket. Many names known throughout Europe have set up on the edge of the larger towns, and you can buy everything under the one roof from a kitchen to a boat or motorbike, to a television or a computer, as well as the week's food and drink supply. Naturally prices are competitive, and on the whole the store's 'own brand' products are worth buying; but if you have two hypers near you it will still be worthwhile to shop around.

If you can't bring yourself to depart from your favourite brands of foodstuffs, you will find that the hypers stock a full range of English and continental brands from corn-flakes to yoghurt. Health food is now allocated a section to itself, and all the muesli, bran, nut and wholefood products can be found there. Once again, you will pay more for your favourite brand but Spanish firms are always quick to see a market, and are fast producing very acceptable alternatives. Whilst on the diet/wholefood subject, it is now almost universal in Spain to show a breakdown of the ingredients in most packaged foodstuffs; in many cases this will include the protein, carbohydrate and calorific values, and in the case of perishables it will also show a sell-by date.

Do-it-yourself equipment, mainly British and German brand names, tends to be expensive, and most long-stay visitors bring their DIY durables such as drills, saws and planes with them. However, hypers do sell all you need to put up shelves, plumb in new sinks, or put up a set of wall lights, and there are many bargains to be had in this range of goods. The Spanish love pretty lighting and many of the ceiling and wall units are indeed most attractive.

Most hypers accept Visa for the purchase of expensive

items such as televisions, videos, furniture and electrical goods, and often there is a free delivery and installation service (*transportaje y montaje gratis*) – so look for the offer, especially if you are buying a new kitchen! There will also most certainly be an 'enquiries and goods return' desk where someone speaks English, so don't be afraid to take something back if it is not to your satisfaction.

Buying clothes
Most long-stay visitors bring a wide range of clothing with them and quite wisely so, for the Spanish seem to produce either exotic, expensive clothing retailed through boutiques and fashion houses, or a great volume of cheap and fashionable wear marketed through stores and hypers, but very little of the middle-of-the-road, durable fashion wear that suits the British taste. Thus it is that you may find yourself, like so many others, going back to the UK occasionally to replenish your wardrobe.

On the other hand, shoes are plentiful and of good quality, and should suit all tastes since they range from exotic hide-skins to the humble espadrilles.

Quick Ways with Conversion
A teacher or a person who spends a lot of time on the continent could miss out this section, for it is intended to help people who find difficulty in thinking in metric terms.

1 Travel
Miles to kilometres. If your car is fitted with a kilometre-per-hour ring inside your mph ring, just read off the distance from that. Yes, it's obvious – but it's surprising how many people sit in their cars and try to work out say, how far 80 kilometres is in miles, when the answer is right in front of them as the 50 mph figure. If your car is not so equipped, divide the kilometre distance by eight and multiply the answer by five; the reverse applies for miles to kilometres. Now, petrol or diesel? There are

roughly 4.5 litres to a gallon, so if petrol is 80 pesetas a litre it is 80 x 4½ = 360 pesetas a gallon, approximately £1.86 at the current exchange rate of 193 pesetas to the £1.00.

Tyre pressure:

22 PSI = 1.52
24 PSI = 1.65 Bar
26 PSI = 1.79
28 PSI = 1.93
30 PSI = 2.07
32 PSI = 2.21

2 Temperature
Some of us will never get used to thinking in centigrade when it comes to the daily temperature, so here is a much quicker way of roughly changing centigrade to fahrenheit. Divide the centigrade temperature by 5 to the nearest 5: eg 38 becomes 40,and 36 becomes 35. Then multiply your answer by 9 and add 32. For example, 26 degrees would become:

25 ÷ 5 = 5 × 9 = 45 + 32 = 77 degrees fahrenheit

Easy, isn't it?

3 Shopping

Rough guides:

Weight:	1 ounce	= 30 grams
	½ ounce	= 230 grams
	1 pound	= 450 grams
Measure:	1 inch	= 2.5 centimetres
	1 foot	= 30 centimetres
	1 yard	= 90 centimetres

The table overleaf shows even quicker ways to convert if you can take a calculator to the shop with you.

Inches to centimetres	multiply by 2.540
Centimetres to inches	0.3937
Feet to metres	0.3048
Metres to feet	3.281
Yards to metres	0.9144
Metres to yards	1.094
Miles to kilometres	1.609
Kilometres to miles	0.6214
Gallons to litres	4.546
Litres to gallons	0.22
Ounces to grams	28.35
Grams to ounces	0.3527
Pounds to kilograms	0.4536
Kilograms to pounds	2.205

Your Health in Spain

Although Spain is considered by many to be a healthy place to live with its ample sunshine and plentiful supply of year-round fresh produce, it still manages to produce its fair quota of medical nasties. The casual visitor may well have discovered some of these, from the famous Spanish tummy to the ubiquitous mosquito with its penchant for transforming you into an advanced case of measles, and all may contribute to making you feel one degree under at times. But before we resort to the medical services, let's look at simple ways of avoiding some of the problems.

Water is a commodity that we cannot live long without, and although the sort that comes out of Spanish taps may be deemed drinkable (*potable*) by hardy natives, to the northern European the harsh lime and salt saturated solution seems to nauseate and bring about a sudden increase in gastric activity. It is true that much is constantly being done to improve local water supplies, but on the whole most people prefer to buy drinking water from the local shop or supermarket at 50 pence for 5 litres. And if you are fortunate enough to have a mountain spring in your area, join the procession of Spaniards with their empty 5-litre containers and top up your supply when needed; but remember – springs, too, can become contaminated, so do *boil* your drinking water before you put it in the fridge.

Ice is another tourist trap: many seem to believe that with liberal quantities of spirits poured over it, ice will miraculously become sterile. But the rule is: when you first arrive, only take iced drinks in the slightly more up-market bars and cafés. As you go along you will find that you gradually build up a resistance to all the local bugs, since you are receiving a low dose with almost everything you consume.

All fresh produce should be thoroughly washed as soon as you get it home; fridges are big in Spain and all salad, vegetables and fruit can be stored in them. Melons should be paid particular attention because of the rather unusual methods of cultivation practised in some parts; as long as the outside skin is intact and thoroughly cleaned you will have little problem, but take care.

Meat should be consumed on the day of purchase, although almost all meat is killed only shortly before sale so it will stand freezing if you do a bit of bulk buying; it does, however, lose a little of its flavour in the process. Chickens should be thoroughly cleaned and well cooked; as in England, they are a regular source of salmonella infections. Milk is nearly all of the UHT type and does not require refrigeration until it is opened. All vacuum-packed food has a sell-by date, so look when you buy bacon, ham and sliced cheeses, etc. Tinned goods may have been on the shelves of small shops for ages, and in areas of high heat and humidity the tin will soon deteriorate. Do not buy tins with rust on them, or tins that have expanded (blown) – there's sure to be something nasty going on inside. Eggs are safe nowadays; they are usually dated, besides which they are used extensively in all forms of Spanish cooking so the turnover is quick.

When buying fish, look for viability in the flesh: it must bounce back when prodded, also the eyes must be clear and obviously the smell must be fresh. Most shellfish and crustaceans are sold live, so there's seldom a problem with these; octopus and squid are almost always fresh-caught.

Mosquito eradication schemes continue without ceasing throughout the year; they are effective up to a point, but do not expect them ever to catch up. If an island like Malta 17 × 8 miles (27 × 13km) still has them, what chance has Spain of winning? And how do you deal with the ones that get away? An evening outside on the terrace or at a barbecue should be accompanied by a liberal application of a good repellent. Your bedroom should be proofed with wind-down nets, or with the very efficient and odourless electrical mosquito units which can be placed in a convenient wall socket. The liquid charged type now gives up to a month's protection. The old-fashioned mosquito nets suspended over the bed provide total protection and a womb-like atmosphere in which to sleep, adored by some and hated by others (mainly claustrophobics). An ioniser will improve the environment of any bedroom, especially in the summer; for those not *au fait* with their use, they change positive ions into negative ones and thereby impart a mountain stream atmosphere to the air. Fans should be used with care during hot summer nights. Many now have timers, so you can avoid having to get up again once you have cooled down; the direct blast of a fan can cause cramps and chills if left on for long periods, so take care.

Moving out-of-doors and into the sunshine we immediately face two major hazards: the destructive effect upon the skin from periods of long exposure; and heat stroke or exhaustion caused by the body's heat regulating mechanism becoming impaired.

The rule is, use high factor protection initially no matter how well you tan; avoid long exposure; and don't spend too long out in the hottest part of the day. Watch the locals: they're under the trees drinking water, not on the beach drinking alcohol and fizzy pop, and they take their main meal in the cool of the day – so, follow their example.

Skin care is very important when you are sweating a lot; tight-fitting waistbands produce prickly heat rash – a nasty, allergic reaction – so wear light coloured and lightweight clothing, and shower or bathe frequently. The use of body oil or lotion will help to replace the natural oils that sweating and washing destroy. Thus by taking care of yourself you need not join the ranks of the costa folk, who bear a strong resemblance to dried fruit.

If you become ill
Should you be taken ill in Spain you will be entitled to use the Spanish government health-service facilities provided you have obtained (1) form E111 if you are staying for 60 days or less, or (2) form E121 if you are retiring or staying long term. You should have taken the form, duly completed, to your local Spanish social security office and they will have issued you with a book of vouchers and a list of doctors and the services you can use. However, most British people do not consider the local facilities adequate enough for their needs, and take out further private health cover through one of the well publicised Spanish schemes. The best available costs only £25.00 a month for whole family cover, and opens the way to more doctors and private clinics with the facility of a private room if you are hospitalised.

A word on chemists (farmacias)
Farmacias in Spain are run by professional dispensing chemists who are still consulted about conditions which would send the average Britisher scuttling off to the doctor. You can purchase a range of drugs including penicillin and other antibiotics, together with many steroids for skin treatment, without prescription and many Spanish and British settlers do pop to the chemist when they're not well. Excessive use of antibiotics and the like does have, of course, the concomitant result of making a patient resistant to their effect, so to take them willy nilly is quite

foolish and may undermine their efficacy when you need them most.

If you do not speak Spanish, take an interpreter with you when you visit the doctor for it is unlikely he will speak a word of English. Do not be surprised if he sends you for hospital tests – these are very popular as new equipment is becoming available to confirm diagnoses. On the matter of treatment it is not unusual for the doctor to prescribe a course of injections rather than orally administered drugs – personally, I feel sure that the Spanish believe it must hurt to work! Also, he may prescribe suppositories as a way of administering a drug; this is also strangely popular.

Admission to a hospital
First, a word or two of warning: if you do live deep in the country you may find it difficult to get a doctor to visit you if you are ill; likewise ambulances, which are mainly privately operated, tend not to carry people who appear insolvent or who are not covered by a private health scheme. The Red Cross (*Cruz Roja*) on the other hand, which is operated entirely by young men who choose this as a form of National Service, will pick anyone up free of any charge; and taxis are also compelled by law to carry medical emergencies to hospital or treatment clinics. And there is one last, typically Spanish innovation if all else fails: any private car may claim precedence on the road when carrying a medical emergency by switching on its hazard lights and displaying a piece of white material from an open window. Needless to say, the penalty for the misuse of this advantage is dire in the extreme.

As when visiting the doctor, you are advised to take an interpreter with you to the hospital as you will have scant chance of finding many staff who speak English. In fact some tour operators have employed bi-lingual nurses to visit when their clients are admitted! The facilities in most Spanish hospitals are equal, or in many cases superior to our own; a lot of government money, as well as money from the private sector, has been put into health care and you can rest assured of good treatment in comfortable conditions.

All hospital patients are expected to be accompanied by someone during their stay, whether they are in a small ward or private room, and this friend or relative must provide for the patient's immediate needs. Nursing staff are for nursing duties only, and there are no auxiliaries or orderlies, only cleaners; therefore your food, washing and bathing must be taken care of by the person accompanying you. Spanish families take it in turns, but in your case there may be only the two of you, so be prepared. In the event of a serious condition, patients are of course 'special-ed' by nursing staff but this does not preclude the need for someone to stay. In the private clinics run by the insurance companies there are suites of rooms with a shower, kitchenette, fridge, couchette, payphone and television; so private insurance is worth a thought if you are prone to a hospitalising condition.

Some UK private health insurance schemes will give you cover for extended periods abroad, and under the terms of most you are entitled to an air ambulance to the UK should you so desire it. The cost of such an operation is prohibitive and currently you won't get any change from £20,000, so it's not a move that many could make without insurance cover.

In Spain you are expected to convalesce at home, and there is a tendency for the patient to be discharged rather sooner than he would be in the UK. One feels that the tradition of extended family support causes the Spanish patient to wish to return to his home as soon as he can, rather than see his condition through to its end in a hospital ward.

There are a few British-run nursing homes springing up on the costas, but they are expensive and so recent a phenomenon that it is difficult to make a balanced judgement on their efficiency.

On a lighter note, if your condition does require on-going physiotherapy it will be carried out at the hospital, so don't do as one Englishman did and visit a massage salon – you will find this is really something completely different!

Education in Spain
Education in Spanish

Education, or rather attendance at a school approved by the government, can and often does start at a very early age. The *Jardin de la Infancia* or more simply *la Guardaria* are privately run, state-approved nursery schools which take children from the age of two to six when formal state education begins. The fees charged at the Guardaria are small and there is informal teaching of music, physical activity, dancing and art. These nursery schools are a boon to the working mother and they are well subscribed, well run, and good value for money.

Compulsory state education begins at six and ends at fifteen. Many of the schools are of the all-in-one type where the child stays, moving through the grades until he leaves or passes on to higher education. Those who achieve the standard of '*Bachillerato*' (about 'O' level) go on to a pre-university course; those who do not are awarded a certificate of attendance and move on to a job training scheme. Many such training schemes are geared to the holiday industry, with day release to colleges where the more academic side of the job is studied – languages, costing, marketing. Then there is 'on the job training' in hotels, restaurants, travel agencies and the ancillary services. On the whole the standard of training is very good and as 1992 approaches one wonders how many more British hotels and restaurants will be keen to employ these well trained and obliging people on their staff.

Many Spaniards send their children to private schools where classes are smaller and the facilities more sophisticated; but even in the state schools parents have to pay for books and equipment, and all extra-curricular activities such as sports clubs and extra classes have to be paid for.

A British child of a parent working in Spain and paying a social security contribution is entitled to attend a Spanish state school free of charge; many less well-off parents take advantage of this, and many mixed marriage children also attend state schools. It is an absolutely foolproof way for the child to acquire excellent Spanish quickly, and as English is now taught in all Spain's schools the child would be well ahead in that subject to compensate for his initial deficiencies in Spanish.

Further education in the Spanish system is provided at universities and in Colleges of Further Education (*Escuelas universitarias*). At college one may take a variety of courses from teaching to hotel management and nursing, and the three-year diploma course entitles the holder to practise in that subject. Universities are found in most major cities, and the four-year degree course (*una licenciatara*) can offer medicine, science and engineering besides other normal degree courses. However, not many grants are available so the burden of payment falls on the student or his parents, and because of this cost many students leave after the first three years when they may be awarded a diploma in their chosen subject. Up to the time of writing many professionals practise with a diploma only, although things are gradually tightening up as EC standards are having to be met.

Education in English

All major cities in Spain have English-speaking schools, and the majority are run by British teachers; all are fee-paying. A list of the main schools together with the subjects they offer and the age range taught is given in the appendix; if you cannot find a school listed in your area, a letter to the nearest one shown will give you the details of any which have perhaps been established in your area more recently. New schools are springing up all the time, but the Spanish government is strict in requiring full proof of qualifications and financial soundness so there need be no fear on that score.

On the whole when compared with the UK, an English-speaking school in Spain has a smaller student population and a lower staff-to-student ratio. In many, and as in the state schools, parents are expected to pay for books and materials as well as pay subscriptions to clubs and activities deemed to extend beyond the curriculum.

The English-speaking schools run by British nationals have joined together to form the National Association of British Schools (NABS) in Spain with their headquarters in Madrid; their membership is scattered throughout the peninsula of Spain, the Balearics and the Canaries, but they are of a universally high standard having been subjected to a period of vetting before acceptance. Their principals meet and discuss syllabuses and curriculum, and staff training is given priority where change is taking place – for example, in the recent transition to GCSE, staff from all over Spain attended a course of familiarisation in Madrid.

The NABS schools offer every type of education from nursery at the age of three, through infant and primary or if preferred, preparatory for public school; then on to secondary and sixth form. Generally, the GCSE syllabus is followed, but many schools also continue with the London or Cambridge 'O' and 'A' levels to prepare their students for university or polytechnic entrance exams. There are many advantages for a child being educated in Spain, provided the right school is chosen. Classes are definitely smaller, and there is less pressure on books and equipment so the student can spend more time establishing his knowledge. Computer studies are very popular, as they are in the UK, but the 'hands on' time is far greater due to the smaller numbers in the classes.

All NABS schools are registered examination centres for all the UK examining boards. In addition to the strictly academic subjects children are also prepared for business and commerce through RSA and Pitman's exams.

Many of the NABS schools take either term-time or weekday boarders, and there is usually a full and lively programme to keep them occupied, the climate readily permitting a wide variety of activities; scouting, guiding, sailing and the Duke of Edinburgh Award training are all pursued with enthusiasm, so there is no fear of a child losing contact with these interests while he is in Spain.

The school term is dictated naturally enough by the weather and the season; hence there are short holidays at Christmas and Easter and very long ones in the summer, usually extending to three months or a little more. Nearly all NABS schools run summer schools and these offer a wide range of activities from visits to the continent, camping, sailing or hiking; pottery, art or language study; photography, and many others – really too numerous to mention.

Other English-speaking schools are run by the Americans and these are found in many major cities throughout Spain. They do not generally belong to the European American Schools Association, and as in the different states in the USA they do tend to operate independently from each other in terms of curriculum, examinations and graduation criteria. Although they take children along the academic study road to the level required for admission to an American university, it must be stated that this standard will by no means satisfy a British university admissions board. On the whole the education is along more liberal lines, and it is the American Advanced Placement examination which provides the final level of achievement.

The international baccalaureate is an examination system which is followed in the English-speaking schools and colleges of other continental countries, whereby the student follows six or seven subjects at an advanced level in his final years; it is not, however, often used in Spain. At the present time it is felt that because of the EC, school examinations are in a state of flux; each country will therefore stick to its own system until a universal examining method is established which will be acceptable throughout the EC membership.

A final word of advice: an early letter, together with a short academic pen-picture from the UK school your child currently attends, will help considerably in establishing a working contact with the English-speaking school in the area of your choice in Spain. Many parents of older children who are well established in British schools, prefer to leave them behind as term-time boarders, and this must be the right decision where the child is at a critical period in preparation for exams. But it must be said that the education offered in Spain is of a high standard, and with the exception of near-examinees, education in Spain should be seriously considered before deciding to leave your child behind in the UK. A child suddenly plunged into boarding-school life with the parents a thousand miles or so away can suffer as much a drop in performance as if he were to change schools, so both factors should be weighed up before a final decision is made.

School Life in Spain

The school year

The school year usually starts in the first week of September; there are six public holidays spread between September and 20 December when the Christmas holiday commences. The new year term starts around the end of the first week in January and goes through until Easter. Those schools which encourage outward-bound activities often organise a skiing holiday of a week's duration in this term. The Easter break is usually of ten or fourteen days and then the summer term goes through until the end of June.

The school day normally starts at 9am; teaching periods are of 45 minutes' duration and continue until 4pm, with an hour off for lunch. Sports, clubs and other extra-mural activities take place after school hours.

As stated above, the courses offered vary from school to school, but in general the GCSE subjects covered are English language, English literature, Spanish, French, German, mathematics, single subject science, double subject sciences and geography. At GCE 'A' level there are mathematics, biology, chemistry, geography, English literature, history, art, history of art, French, Spanish and German. Most English-speaking schools have a multi-national population, and the opportunity to follow language courses is not to be missed. A friend of the author has no less than nine nationalities currently attending his school and on occasions there have been even more.

Fees and expenses
Not all schools require their students to wear uniform, but where they do the cost must be added to the figures given below.

Day Students

	Kindergarten	to	Sixth form
Tuition	£1,000	to	£3,370
Registration and book rental	£100	to	£200
Emergency/damage deposit	£50		

Insurance
Most schools subscribe to a block insurance scheme which covers accidents both in school and on school sponsored activities.

Scholarships and grants
Lack of sufficient funds should not deter parents from applying for a place for their child. A number of scholarships are awarded each year, and there are grants provided to help people meet the fees – depending, of course, on their circumstances.

Performance
With smaller classes and more individual attention, children will inevitably achieve better results in examination. Of those taking GCSE and 'A' level exams at one school last year a pass rate of 85 per cent was recorded, and university entrance grades of A to C were achieved by no less than 75 per cent of those taking 'A' level. This

means, of course, that there is a far higher percentage of pupils who may go on to university or further education, and from the age of 13 or 14 onwards career counselling is given high priority, particularly once subject choices have been made.

Homework

Since most schools in Spain arrange their terms to fit the truncated school year, homework has an essential place in the student day and the following programme of homework is usually expected of pupils:

11 years old	90 minutes, 5 times a week
12 years old	120 minutes, 5 times a week
13/14 years old	150 minutes, 5 times a week
15/17 years old	180 minutes, 5 times a week

Failure to show sufficient effort may result in academic probation being imposed, and a progress card is marked by each teacher throughout the school day until performance improves.

Discipline other than that mentioned above focuses on a system of warnings – discussion first, and finally suspension. Parental involvement is invariably sought when difficulties arise, and where possible counselling is carried out by the year teachers concerned.

Boarders

Many of the English-speaking schools take term-time boarders, and a price guide is given here to indicate some of the costs entailed:

Boarding fees, ages 11 to 17

Boarding and tuition	£7,500
Registration and book rental	£200
Emergency/damage deposit	£600

The emergency/damage deposit covers the following needs:

medical emergencies, breakages and damage, extra-curricular activities, excursions, urgent travel and laundry.

These guide prices are based upon a survey of only a few British-run schools, thus they should only be taken as a rough guide when budgeting – further information will readily be offered by the school of your choice. A list of addresses of British schools is given in the appendix (see pp186–8).

Insurances

Like most people moving out to Spain you will probably have some form of current personal insurance running when you leave the UK, be it a life or an endowment policy; and provided you inform the company of your change of address and your UK bank keeps paying the premiums, nothing more need be done on that count until you die or the policy matures.

Private health insurance cover, however, will not usually be transferable if you are taking up residence in Spain. Most companies only allow holiday cover within their terms and this is usually limited to so many days per year; they will not cover you if you actually make your home abroad. So to find out how you stand, write to your insurers well in advance and advise them what you are proposing to do, stating the period you intend staying out of the UK; they will then let you know if cover can be provided. Private health cover is considered essential by British residents in Spain, and many Spanish firms give very satisfactory family cover for around £25 per month. IMECO is the most well known, and they will provide you with a list of doctors on their payroll and a list of private clinics where you can receive in-patient treatment (see also p79 for health care in Spain). All the usual health cover is provided under these schemes, including family practitioner care, specialists, consultants, X-rays, laboratory tests, scans and hospital investigations, surgery and convalescence; some schemes even include dental emergencies in their cover, although it is advisable to get a full translation of the policy before marching off for treatment to ensure that you are covered.

Insurance of personal and household effects can be obtained from British-franchised insurers in Spain, Sun Alliance and Guardian Royal Exchange to name but two. However, these firms are Spanish-administered offshoots, and all their policies and certification documents are therefore produced in Spanish from their Madrid head offices. Hopefully you will find a British agent acting for them in your area, so any problems that occur can at least be sorted out in your mother tongue. Where property has been burgled, all insurers will require a police certificate stating that there was clear evidence of a break-in, eg physical damage to the property and the exact value of the property stolen. You will need the assistance of a reasonably fluent Spanish speaker at the police station, so go prepared if you are not fluent yourself. The cover given by the British firms is good, and you should not have problems recovering the cost of your stolen items. The author cannot, however, vouch for the credibility of the Spanish insurers as none are personally known to him, however, their premiums are almost identical with those charged in the UK and cover is the same, with new for old and all risks being allowed on payment of a slightly higher premium. If you enjoy sport and play a lot it is worth getting yourself insured for personal liability; accidents do occur on the ski slopes and even when playing golf and the premium charged is very small.

When insuring boats, or any other item that may be kept a distance away from your property, you should seek advice from your insurers. Outboard engines and the like should always be detached and stored at home where possible – they are a target for thieves in Spain just as much as in the UK.

Building insurance is rather complicated in that many people live in communities and complexes where buildings are insured by the community, and the premium is charged in the community charges. If you are lucky enough to live in a private house on your own land it is certainly worth taking out a building insurance, to cover for example a wall falling down or a water tank bursting its sides. Building in no way comes up to our UK standards, and at various times one hears of terraces collapsing and subsidence claiming hillside developments. Things are now improving and building regulations are being more firmly applied, but they are not retrospective and many lovely old houses were built long before these rules came into effect. So if in doubt, get a survey done and then insure, quoting the surveyor by name – he will then have to stand by his report.

A final word on insurances: don't forget that you can claim back the unused portion of any premium which you have already paid for cover in the UK, so start the wheels rolling well before you leave – many insurers are renowned for their slowness in paying out. Also, make sure that you inform the insurers of any UK property you are leaving unoccupied for more than two months, or you may find that in the event of a break-in or a burst pipe you are not covered even though you have paid your premiums.

The English Church
Anglican Churches in Europe
English churches and congregations have been established on the continent since before the Reformation, and the number of these grew to such an extent that in 1633 all the congregations of the Church of England in all foreign countries were placed under the jurisdiction of the Bishop of London. Anglican dioceses and then provinces were later formed in all parts of the world outside the UK; the Diocese of Gibraltar was founded in 1842 to take over pastoral care of the chaplaincies and congregations of southern Europe and Turkey. And in 1883 the Bishop of London appointed a suffragon bishop, who was later given the title of Bishop of Fulham, to supervise northern and central Europe. From 1920 these amalgamated, and the jurisdiction of all

northern and central Europe together with the Diocese of Gibraltar was committed to the episcopal care of one bishop, the Bishop of Fulham and Gibraltar. Since 1980 a single diocese has been formed with the title of The Diocese of Gibraltar in Europe, when it became the forty-fourth diocese of the Church of England.

The Anglican Communion maintains friendly relations with all the major Christian churches on the continent, and is in full communion with the Lusitanian Church (Portugal) and the Spanish Episcopal Reformed Church (which in 1980 were both accepted as churches of the Anglican Communion), and also with the Old Catholic Church, following the Bonn Agreement of 1931.

There are eight archdeaconries, and the one concerning residents in Spain also covers the western Mediterranean, Portugal, Morocco, Madeira and the Canary Islands. The Cathedral Church is that of the Holy Trinity in Gibraltar.

That is the brief historical background; now we shall look at the church in action in Spain.

The Anglican Church in Spain
The Anglican Church is well served in most of the tourist areas, and in the British residential areas of Spain. The Bishop of Gibraltar in Europe, The Rt Rev John R. Satterthwaite tends his flock, officiates at confirmations and spends much time visiting his diverse ministries – Barcelona, Bilbao, Costa Blanca, Fuengirola, Costa del Sol, Madrid, Malaga and the Balearics all have their established churches. Congregations are on the whole large and enthusiastic, and much interest is taken in church affairs and fund raising. There is also a lot of co-operation between the Anglican and the established Spanish Catholic churches and visitors from either denomination are welcome to take mass if they are a communicant member of another persuasion, or to receive an altar blessing if they have not been confirmed. This is a long way along the road to church unity, when only twenty years back the children of Spanish families on their way to mass were

shown the Anglican churches and warned that the devil was at work there!

In a wider context the church also provides a support for those members of the British community who have run into problems, or who simply needed occupation. If asked, the priest will visit the sick in their homes, and give communion, and he will frequently visit the local hospital if a British resident is there having treatment. Hospital visitors, often self-appointed, do excellent work ferrying people for appointments and helping with translations where needed. People have time on their hands here if they are retired, and many charitable souls enjoy this helping role – unpaid, but never unthanked. Furthermore, the church rooms are often used by groups such as Alcoholics Anonymous to hold therapy meetings – a lot of good counselling work is being carried out in this field and the results are satisfying. There is also the Salvation Army, established in many towns; in their traditional way they hold services and run thrift shops and generally carry on their good works – though local laws prevent them canvassing the resort taverns with their collecting boxes.

In some towns such as Palma the free churches have integrated with the Anglican community and come under the one roof, which seems to be a success. Other religious groups such as the Born Again Christians have established themselves as permanent residents – one has even taken over a small resort hotel, and seems to get a lot of support from all over Europe judging by the car licence plates parked outside.

Charity work is often linked to the churches, and each bazaar or jumble sale brings a mountain of second-hand goods and an army of willing helpers. The Lions, the Rotary Club, the Round Table and the Masons all have their established groups carrying on as if they were in the UK with charity work and gala evenings for their members. Furthermore, many will be pleased to hear that the canine defence league, the cats' protection league and various other animal welfare groups are all well established and doing nicely. All in all the community atmosphere is enhanced by the distance from the UK and with inevitably more time on their hands people manage to put much more into their interests, unhampered as they are by the constraints of a UK working week.

Societies working in the diocese also include the Intercontinental Society, the Mediterranean Mission to Seamen (whose president is the Bishop of Gibraltar in Europe), the Churches of Scotland and the Methodist Churches in Europe.

There is also a diocesan gazette which is published quarterly; the annual subscription is £1.00 which also covers postage to any part of Spain.

The addresses of all the above together with names of contacts, can be found in the appendix (pp188–90); you will also find a list of the Anglican churches in principal towns in Spain, to help you.

The Lord's Prayer in Spanish:

Padre nuestro
Que estas en los cielos
Santificado sea tu nombre
Venga a nosotros tu reino
Hagase tu voluntad
Asi en la tierra como en el cielo
El pan nuestro de cada dia danosle hoy
Y perdonanos nuestras deudas
Asi como nosotros perdonamos a nuestros deudores
Y no nos dejes caer en la tentacion
Mas libranos del mal
Porque tuyo es el reino, el poder y la gloria
Por siempre Señor
Amen.

Marriage, Birth and Death

Quite a lot of British girls marry their Spanish holiday boyfriends and appear to integrate reasonably well into

Spanish society, rearing their 2.4 children who will enjoy the added advantages of being bilingual and able to share in both cultures, as long as the British partner's family maintains regular contact. Furthermore, the children of mixed marriages do on the whole tend to start with one foot up the ladder in terms of job prospects in Spain; their fluent English opens many doors in both the service industries and selling.

Any social adjustment in such a marriage falls mainly on the woman, who not only has to learn a language, but must adapt to the traditional Spanish family way of life, including a husband who – if a recent national Spanish paper is to be believed – is still essentially *macho* and chauvinistic. The survey revealed that whilst only 50 per cent of Spanish husbands maintained that housework is only for women, 87 per cent never do the ironing, and 77 per cent never wash any clothes. They appear, when questioned, to be on the side of egalitarianism, but in fact are little changed. Being *macho* in the bedroom is important to them, and they also believe that sex is more important for men than women; on the subject of infidelity, men thought their 'affairs' were unimportant – but few had the same view when questioned about women straying!

In almost all cases the children are brought up as Catholics; education depends a lot on the parents' socio-economic group, though there is a tendency to opt for private education where it is financially possible.

British men, on the other hand, do not get as much exposure to Spanish girls because of the social constraints placed upon the girls by their parents and peers. Of course they meet as disco partners and on the beaches, but British boys are not the scalp-hunters that the Spanish men are – and after all, there are a lot of very attractive British girls about the resorts, so why bother?

Getting married
In Spain you can get married either at your embassy or before a Spanish judge. For marriage in a church the

certificate is obtained from the nearest town hall, and in Spain both parties must prove that they are legally free to marry. In the case of a UK divorcee, a copy of the certificate of divorce, legalised by the Spanish Consul in the UK, must be produced. In fact divorcees are not currently allowed to marry in any Spanish church, though this is under review for certain circumstances such as non-consummation of the previous marriage.

Of course, there are advantages in marrying a Spanish national, particularly when obtaining work – if your name is Garcia Lopez it will get a quicker journey through the administrative machine than if it were Thompson or Brown. After ten years, the foreigner may apply for Spanish nationality if he so chooses. The children of the mixed marriage can take up either or both nationalities, and the consul will advise upon this.

Birth

As in so many other things, the procedure for having a baby in Spain is not quite the same as that in the UK. There is no ante-natal organisation, as such, as in the UK, although the ante-natal facilities are there and they are excellent – it is up to the individual to use them. Examinations, ultra-sonic scans and blood checks are all carried out, and the woman will be admitted into the government hospital or private clinic depending on whether she subscribes to a private health scheme or not.

Once again, the mother is expected to be attended by a relative or friend during her confinement; and mother and child are discharged to home somewhat earlier than in the UK. Any post-natal follow-up for either the mother or the child must be initiated by the mother, as there are no health visitors or post-natal clinics as such. The baby's birth must be registered at the local town hall, and from then on he/she is entitled to all the facilities offered by the Spanish state, including education and health care. Some British women do go back to the UK to have their babies, for reasons, they feel, of security and so the child is eligible

(Previous page) *Still life, Spanish style*

(Above) *Beach life* . . .
(Below) *. . . but not all beaches are bursting with holidaymakers*

(Left) *Setting up for the day*

(Below) *Cheeses and hams in an open air market*

(Bottom) *Nets must be mended*

(Overleaf) *Traditional Spanish courtyard*

(Left, top) *Castles in Spain*

(Left, middle) *A traditional hacienda*

(Left, bottom) *Tasteful urban development*

(Above) *Spaghetti Western town*

(Below) *Relics of the Spanish Inquisition, evidence of man's inhumanity to man*

Rooms with a view

for a British birth certificate; it is a matter of choice and depends on the individual. The Spanish medical facilities are certainly equal, if not superior to those in the UK – but there's nothing like having the family around at certain times, is there?

Dealing with a death
If someone dies in Spain and the circumstances are not open to question, the local funeral service will deal with all the arrangements, including obtaining the death certificate. However, you will have to decide whether you wish the deceased to be buried in Spain or transported back to the UK for interment. The latter is a very expensive operation unless the body is first cremated, and to add to the difficulty there are very few crematoriums in Spain since it is a Catholic country.

The deceased may be buried in Spain in any municipal cemetery, and the current cost of a funeral is comparable to one in the UK; it is perhaps worth considering an insurance to cover these costs which are rising annually. Both UK and Spanish insurance companies will issue policies for this purpose.

If you hold a joint bank account with the deceased you would do well to close that account immediately and open another in your name only, as the Spanish have a rather worrying habit of freezing all things until probate has been established. You should always recruit the help of your solicitor whilst the will is being proved (for tax liabilities, see pp160–1 on inheritance laws).

In parts of Spain where ground space is at a premium the bodies of the dead are sealed into sort of high-rise tombs, with a plaque on each entrance giving the relevant details. In some regions the duration of stay in a high-rise tomb is limited to a number of years – sometimes five – after which the body (or rather the skeleton) is placed in a large communal tomb and the plaque attached to the wall. The reasons given for this strange ritual vary; on the islands, where it is practised most, it is generally put down to the

105

problem of having so little room. There is also a folklore belief that a family member must be at the disinterment to certify that the body is still there – the root reason for this is involved with the afterlife, and again it varies. Obviously, this procedure does not happen to people who are placed in private tombs which have been paid for in perpetuity.

These points are made purely to guide you should you be contemplating burial in Spain. One thing is for sure, you will have a lot of visitors around you on All Saints' Day (*Dia los Todos Santos*) on 1 November, when the Spanish honour their dead by meeting as a family at the cemetery, often keeping vigil for the day. Many tomb plaques incorporate a photograph of the deceased as an added reminder of who they were. The most wealthy Spanish families own family mausoleums which are grand buildings within the grounds of the cemetery where their dead are interred; one of these known to the author has a twenty-four hour guard.

Crime in Spain

The tabloids love the banner headlines 'Costa del Crime', which usually refers to the so-called enclave near Marbella in southern Spain where all the big-time criminals are supposed to be living the life of Reilly. Of course this tale is very far from the truth; no criminal of any repute would be so silly as to take up residence in an area notorious for its criminal population, and the real Mr Biggs, if he is on Spanish soil and actively engaged in any form of crime, is much more likely to be caught, and extradited to face the charges. Therefore one must conclude that people who claim to be villains are more probably ex-car dealers and 'Minder' type entrepreneurs whose crime involves undeclared taxes and unpaid VAT rather than 'bank jobs'!

Spain's attitude to criminal activity of any form is quite firm and each year the budget allotted to crime detection and law enforcement is increased. More recently, mobile interview vans are being used in areas where crime is prevalent and this helps considerably in speeding up the process of catching criminals who would otherwise have time to flee.

A study of crime statistics over the past ten years will show that there has been a vast increase in crimes against the person and his property, and the reason for this must be related to the similar rise in similar crimes in the UK and northern Europe. In spite of Spain's long-season holiday industry, she still has a very high unemployment rate and this, coupled with the fact that there is very little government support for the unemployed, means that the only option that appears to exist for the person out of a job is to engage in some form of illegal activity to earn enough to live.

Holiday homes, which are increasing rapidly in number and for the greater part of the year are left unoccupied, present a perfect target for the petty thief. There are scores of break-ins every day, not only in the off-season either, but often whilst the owners are on the beach, swimming in their pool or even watching television. Hot weather encourages people to leave windows and doors open, and the opportunist thief who spies some attractive and portable item such as a camera, binoculars, radio, watch or money will take a chance, hop through the window, pinch it and be off in a flash. And it must be emphasised here that very few insurance companies will pay out if there is no visible sign of a physical break-in. It is because of this vulnerability that people with holiday homes tend to live in communities and urban developments which are patrolled by security men, paid for in their community charges. The property in the idyllic site on a hill, removed from noise and other properties, becomes a perfect target when the owners are away and it is not uncommon to hear of the same one being broken into two or three times a year; what this must do to the insurance premium one dreads to think (see also pp59–62, Buying a Property in Spain).

Blocks of flats are less susceptible, except for the lower floors or those now fashionable where there are only low walls separating each terrace. Penthouses can be vulnerable, too, if part of the roof of the building is set aside as a communal solarium. Even full-time porters on the ground floor reception area cannot be expected to recognise every owner; and it is made even more difficult for them when flats are let to family and friends, or in some cases let commercially. The truth of the matter is that all properties are vulnerable, but some more so than others. On the other hand, it is worth a mention that there are British people who live in villages away from the coast who never have to lock a door or close a window, such is the trust among the community; but these pockets of 'old' culture are getting more scarce, particularly as foreigners spread away from the costas.

Here are a few well tried tips to deter the burglar: wrought iron is cheap and very attractive, and grills can be made for accessible windows and doors at a reasonably low cost – they make a break-in almost impossible, and in many cases attract a reduced insurance premium. Drainpipes can be wound with barbed wire at some point, and painted white so it doesn't show. Sophisticated alarms can be fitted, although these are of little use if no-one is around to hear them go off – sirens have been known to wail for days on end up in the hills. An alarm box placed in an eye-catching position even without the expensive system may work just as well, particularly if the thief has a less difficult target as a choice. If you don't want the expense of wrought iron work, screws can be inserted in your shutter catches to make them impossible to open without force.

Never leave notes on the door in any language which indicates your absence. Arrange for someone to visit your property regularly if you are away, and ensure that they empty your mail box. Never mark your property keys with your name or address, and if you lose them it is best to change the locks just in case. Have a good strong safe built into your property if you have to keep valuables or money in any quantity; thieves will rarely bother with it as they prefer things which are easily transportable and easily sellable.

Currently there is a lot of fraud involving credit cards and travellers' cheques, so take particular care of these. If your car is of a popular make it is worth having a cheap alarm system fitted, as cars are regularly stolen on mainland Spain and are difficult to trace – a conspicuous alarm system is a good deterrent. Wheel-locking bolts are also a good idea if you drive a popular make of car.

As a person, you may well be vulnerable to attack by muggers in many of the bigger towns and resort areas. Groups of young Spaniards and delinquent foreigners, usually involved in drug-taking, often roam the less populated streets and are likely to snatch anything you may be carrying, be it a handbag or a camera, sometimes in broad daylight. You should *always* let your possession go; many of these people are desperate and carry knives, and it is not worth getting stabbed. If you are attacked, get to the police immediately and given them a description; but more importantly, keep to well populated areas and don't carry much of value if you can avoid it. And a little tip for ladies: bag-snatchers sometimes operate on scooters and will take shoulder bags as they drive by – so carry your bag on the inside of the pavement if you can, and don't go out decked up like a Christmas tree with gold necklaces and brooches as this is bound to attract muggers.

If you return to your property and find it has been broken into, do *not* go in alone as the thieves may still be there – find some hefty neighbour, or better still, get the police.

The main points to remember are really common sense: don't take chances, though protect yourself and your property as best you can; a good dog is an excellent deterrent whether he is on a lead with you, or roaming your property unchained, but remember: a dog is a lot of work, and needs a lot of attention, and it is equally criminal to leave it chained up all day to bark its head off.

This may all seem to present a picture of doom and

gloom, and if this is so, I am sorry. Crime in Spain is rising, but no more so than in most other places in Europe – there is little, if anything, written here that would not apply in any major city in the UK. If it's any consolation, in the twelve years we have been property owners in Spain we have never had a thing stolen, nor have we ever felt threatened; but it is always better to be safe, and aware of the fact that these things do happen to some people and also that they are happening more frequently.

6
Sport and Leisure

Sports For All

Whether your reason for coming to Spain is to retire or to have a long holiday, then you have certainly chosen the right place – the balance between climate and amenity makes it the perfect spot to enjoy a vast range of sports and pursuits. First we will consider the more physically active person, for without doubt this must be his haven.

Sports complexes are springing up in many of the resort areas of Spain and the cost to the resident is small; he is fully entitled to use something he has contributed towards through his local taxes. A standard charge of just £20.00 per year can therefore give a whole family access to indoor swimming, gymnasium, and health and fitness equipment of a very high standard. There is a high standard of supervision; also before the prospective participant even embarks on a fitness course or aerobics, he will have to obtain a medical certificate (given free) from a nominated practitioner to say he is fit to follow the course. Badminton, squash, tennis, archery and boule are all becoming available at these centres. People living outside the district may use the facilities, but the charges for individual sports are quite high.

Cycling is very popular in Spain and there are many well established clubs who would be happy to let you join their ranks if you have the energy and the nerve to travel their mountain routes.

Golf is expensive everywhere, but nevertheless very popular. There are very few private clubs, and most courses are owned by syndicates with annual or daily fees charged for play. However, becoming an annual fee-paying member can mean a long wait – in some areas it takes years – so enquire around some time before you intend moving and get your name on the waiting list. Fees range from £350 to £3,000 per year depending on the club, and from £15 to £100 per round for the non-member. Playing with a member often means a reduction of between 30 or 40 per cent in the green fee. On the whole the courses are excellent and beautifully maintained. In the heat of the summer you will find the courses of the south almost empty even if you personally have the stamina to play; but once the winter comes you must book your tee time at least the day before if you wish to play.

As well as at the municipal complexes, the tennis player will find courts available at most hotels, and upon payment of a few hundred pesetas these will usually allow you to use their courts, even if you are not a resident. Tennis coaching complexes run by big-name players are available to those with a high standard of play and with the money to pay the fees; some luxury hotels have sports coaches on their staff, too, so it is worth asking around if you are keen to improve your game.

Squash is slowly catching on in Spain; it is available in the municipal ventures and in small squash clubs which are springing up in the larger towns. The standard of play is generally low, so if you are a reasonable club player your services may be useful as a coach!

With her miles of coastline, Spain is a natural haven for the water sports' enthusiast – whether he is a humble air-bed paddler or an off-shore yacht racer, he will surely find that Spanish waters are his Shangri-la.

All major ports have their boating clubs (*club nautico*), although these are not cheap to join, and mooring and harbour fees are prohibitive – you would be well advised to make a lot of enquiries before you bring your boat out to Spain. For instance, a 26–33ft (8–10m) mooring can cost £25,000 *plus* an annual rental; and that is not as high as some go! Even so, the competition and enthusiasm for water sports – and especially sailing – is very keen, and in many of Spain's harbours and marinas many millions of pounds' worth of beautiful ocean-going craft may be seen at any one time. Class dingy-racing takes place all year round on the Mediterranean coast. Yacht-racing, both round the buoys and long-haul, is confined to the season from April to October, after which many of the ocean-going racers leave for the West Indies; crewing is always a possibility (see pp139–40, Job Opportunities).

Water activities other than sailing seem to be carried out on a more individual basis; ski schools are profit-making Costa beach business, and so too are the diving schools that now advertise courses. Always ask to see the credentials of anyone offering a diving course and ensure that there is a facility in the area for decompression should it be needed – don't be fobbed off with the excuse that the course does not involve going deep enough to merit this, as accidents do happen.

Schnorkelling and fishing both from boat and shore provide a lot of fun, if not a lot of fish. Away from the resort areas the seas are clear and clean and an afternoon spent just gazing through a face mask, or dangling a bait on a hook and watching the fish ignore it, can provide a very pleasant way to pass the time.

Away from the coast, Spain opens up a veritable box of delights with a vast variety of scenery, flora and fauna to observe; so, if we prefer not to join the cycling fraternity, with bursting lungs and nerves of steel, how best do we avail ourselves of this natural amenity?

The Great Outdoors

Many of the vast tracts of sparsely inhabited Spain have been designated National Parks, with both their flora and fauna protected by statute enforced by teams of wardens. Groups of ecologists have also set out to monitor the effects of development in terms of road building and over-use of these areas by campers and climbers, and to note the effect on the wildlife. So before you venture off into these regions be sure that you have a clear idea of what you may and may not do. Maps and route guides are available at the information centres open in the season; scenic routes are shown, together with permitted camping sites and refuges.

The Picos de Europa area (mentioned on p26) has its Covadenga National Park. Then there is the Cerdesa National Park in Aragon, which perhaps offers the greatest variety of scenery and wildlife as it takes in part of the Pyrenees; accommodation is plentiful, and routes are well marked. Part of it forms the border between France and Spain so be careful to follow the marked routes as things can be a little sensitive along this divide. To the east, Catalonia offers the Aigues Tortes National Park; whilst in La Mancha and Andalucia are the famous bird sanctuaries so often featured in BBC television wildlife programmes, which offer endless enjoyment to bird-watchers and naturalists alike. In these wet lands, however, do be prepared to suffer the onslaught of the ubiquitous mosquito that runs amok from dusk till dawn; to carry out a control programme here would certainly tip the natural balance away from the bird-life. The Tablas de Daimiel National Park is in La Mancha, and to the south-west the Donun Reserve extends through the wet lands of Seville and Huelva.

There is so much to see that it would take an average lifetime to exhaust all Spain's natural regions; if you are so minded, get a good guide book, plan your routes well and just enjoy as many of the wonders of Spain as you can.

Skiing is *not* the chaotic, crowded-slope and après-ski affair that it is in regions further north. Spain has ski resorts scattered throughout its many mountain regions, from the Picos de Europa in the west to the Pyrenees which include the popular ski resorts of Baqueira-Beret near Lerida, as far as Candanchi in Aragon. In the mountainous southern region of the Sierra Nevada you will find Solynieve, which must be the most popular area. During the winter months you will get a ski piste report for all regions after the 8.30pm news on TVE 1. Remarkably,

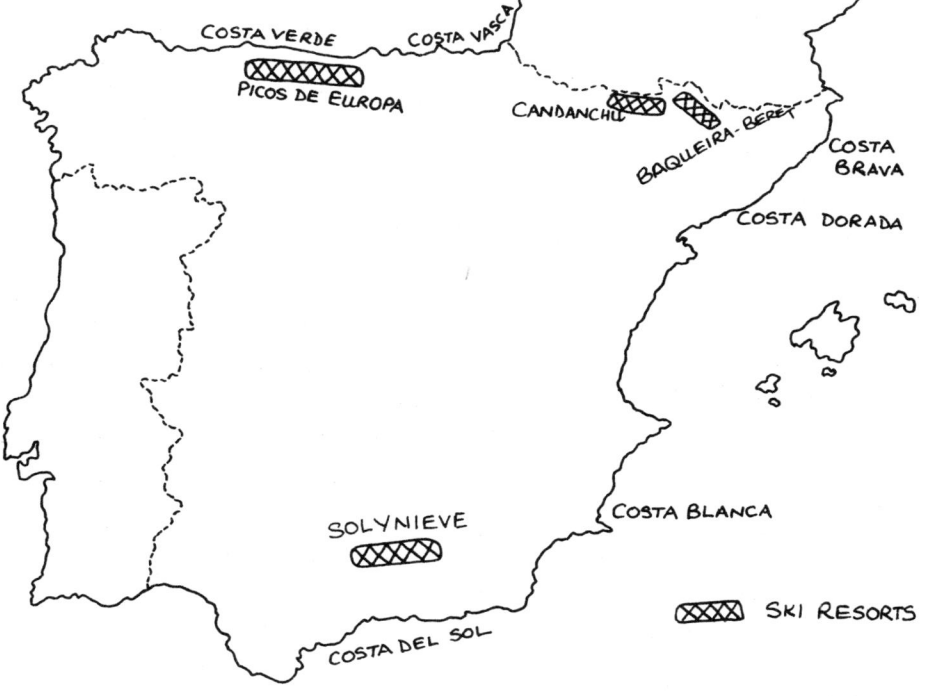

COSTA VERDE   COSTA VASCA

PICOS DE EUROPA

CANDANCHU   COSTA
BAQUEIRA-BERET   BRAVA

COSTA DORADA

COSTA BLANCA

SOLYNIEVE

⊠⊠⊠ SKI RESORTS

COSTA DEL SOL

Costas and ski resorts

in the north of Spain you may ski as late in the year as April, on pistes of 3,300ft (1,000m) or more, and of course Andorra has snow till late June. The cost of skiing in Spain is much lower than at the continental resorts; accommodation and food are also much more reasonably priced, and you do avoid those noisy and at times reckless crowds.

The mountaineer and modest climber will obviously find a wealth of challenges throughout Spain both in terms of difficulty of ascent, and in the variety of geological rock structure. Do not, however, expect the rescue back-up service that you get in the rest of Europe. Spain has enough to be getting on with developing her country, and is unwilling to spend money on manpower on such luxuries as mountain rescue services. Climbing is an individual affair in Spain, and as such is carried out at your own risk. If there is a club where you intend going, do seek local knowledge before setting off – remember the wildlife does include brown bears and the odd wolf, neither of which take kindly to being disturbed when they have young. So, take care!

A word on hunting, for with so much game about it is obvious that hunting does go on; and anyway it would be difficult to eradicate it, with such large tracts of uninhabited land around. Some thirty to forty million hectares are designated as land on which hunting can take place, and in their seasonal turn such game as partridge, pigeon, dove, rabbit, hare, goat, deer, chamois and wild boar all have their allotted season. But don't for one moment expect that all you do is dive into the nearest gun shop and buy a weapon and shells, and race off to wreak havoc with nature. Shooting is strictly controlled. There are many hunting clubs, and there is a government-controlled Spanish Hunting Federation which is responsible for all matters to do with game and its pursuit. Licences are needed for weapons, insurance is compulsory, and shooting regions are patrolled to ensure that nothing is shot out of season. If shooting game is your sport, then you are advised to join a club if at all possible; you will then be guided through the regulations as to where and what and when you may shoot – otherwise you could very well end up gazing at a magistrate.

Gun regulations
As a UK citizen you may import your own personal firearm; however, before you leave the UK you must take your current firearm certificate to the Spanish Consulate, together with a photocopy and your passport. He will then issue you with an import certificate; on arrival in Spain you must take this to your local police headquarters for scrutiny. They will then issue a Spanish gun permit, provided you can show good reason for wanting to hold such a weapon, eg hunting, sport-target, skeet shooting etc. The rest should be plain sailing, provided you (a) join a hunting or sport-shooting club, and (b) get a permit to shoot over a particular tract of land. You will also need to show that you have adequate facilities for the safe storage of the weapon on your property. Finally, the signs you will often see hanging on forest trees with '*coto privado de caza*' mean 'private hunting area': so keep clear!

Fishing
Fishing is also a popular pastime; whilst the Spanish coasts may well be fished out (except for the prolific grey mullet which doesn't seem to take any bait at all), the inland rivers, lakes and waterways can provide splendid sport to any keen angler. Trout, bream and bass are caught in all the large rivers that flow into the Atlantic, and along the Cantabrian coast salmon may provide sport for the lucky linesman. As with shooting, you will need a licence, and also guidance as to where and when and what you may fish; the Spanish Department of Agriculture and Fishing will provide you with all the information you need.

The addresses of all the organisations and federations

controlling the activities mentioned in this chapter are
listed in the appendix, pp185–6.

Other leisure activities

For the less active leisure seeker too, Spain has a box of
delights; whole colonies of writers and painters, poets and
musicians, sculptors and their disciples can be found in
many parts of Spain living happy, contented lives whilst
making enough to enjoy a modest life-style. For the bud-
ding artist the scope is enormous; the quality of light is
good throughout most of the year, and a plentiful supply
of artists' materials can be bought at fair prices, so the
country is yours. Many of the English-speaking schools
run summer and winter art classes for adults, and it is
surprising how many people find a hidden talent at almost
any age. Photography is also a very rewarding hobby in
Spain, but be warned: materials are best bought and
processed in the UK. If normally you use a (British) commercial processor, bring a pack of his mailing envelopes
with you and send them back with friends to post in the
UK; the finished prints can come back by the same route
if you have frequent visitors.

Language learning can be a very rewarding way of
spending your leisure time, especially in Spain where
there are many nationalities living together. As with art,
the English schools also run language classes; and there is
a plethora of mini-language schools advertising their services – though mainly teaching Spanish, it must be said.

Americans and British do seem to be attracted to clubs,
and so the British, or more commonly the British American
Club does tend to arise where two or three are gathered
together. Without doubt these clubs provide a social focus;
they usually have a library, all the English and American
papers are delivered, games such as snooker and bridge,
informal dances and get-togethers all help the community
to get to know each other. They also serve as an important
centre of information to those who have recently arrived
and want to know how, or where, to get things done. Many

run beginners' Spanish courses, and since these are either free, or certainly cheap, they encourage pensioners on a fairly tight budget to learn at least to get by in the Spanish language without the expense of going to a language school. Lessons in a language school are currently around £2.50–£3.00 per hour in a class of ten, and at least six months is needed to really get by in the language; and usually the older you are, the more difficult it becomes (see pp168–71 for an introduction to the language, with a shopping guide etc).

Cooking and Eating

With such a range of climate, together with the incredible resourcefulness of the Spanish people, it is little wonder that each growing season is followed by yet another; strawberries, tomatoes and cucumber, lettuce and beans – an enormously wide range of vegetables and soft fruits are always available, and without the sharp seasonal price rises that one is accustomed to in northern Europe. The cook can therefore plan ahead throughout the year without seasonal constraint upon his menu, and the enthusiastic shopper can easily get carried away. Ideally, if you have the time it is best to shop on the day you need the food, for then it will indeed be at its freshest. Even if you work, you should be able to do this, as food shops are open from 8.30am to 8.30pm in most towns and villages; if you cannot, then choose your produce carefully. Avocados ripen overnight unless they are kept in the fridge, and in fact all soft fruit and vegetables go off very quickly especially if bumped or bruised. The giant lettuce (*lechuga*) weighing up to a kilo are best separated, washed and kept in the 'crisp' compartment of the fridge until required. Tomatoes are of two varieties: the small ones – 'Canary' – popular in England in the winter; and the cheaper, more flavoursome giant Spanish tomato, best chosen slightly greenish-yellow (*ensalada*) for salads, and red and solid (*madura*) for cooking. Tomato purée (*frito*) is sold in tins or jars under such brand names as Solis; it is an excellent combination of tomatoes, onions and oil which has been partly cooked, and which serves as a dressing or a thickening agent for sauces or stews.

Garlic (at just over £1.00 a kilo) is added to most dishes in Spain, and a conversation at close quarters with any Spaniard will soon remind you of this. However, most British settlers soon seem to acquire a taste for it and from then on never smell it except in the dishes they are cooking or eating. The health-giving qualities of garlic have been written about for centuries; several hundreds of years BC, Hippocrates recommended garlic for a variety of ills, and recent findings have shown that garlic does reduce cholesterol and other fatty acids in the bloodstream thus keeping the arteries free and the blood pressure down.

Spain produces about 190,000 tons of garlic annually, and those unique garlic plaits can be seen in delicatessens and health food stores the world over. Spain is also the world's largest producer of olive oil, and is therefore able to retail a baffling variety of oil products at very reasonable prices. The important thing is to find out *what* you are buying as the fancy label and the special offer price may not be the oil you want. The government has now sanctioned the use of the denomination of origin to help identify the high quality oils; the names to look for are 'Sierra de Segura' from Jaen, and 'Borjas Blancas' from Lerida. The oil is classified according to a degree of acidity – the higher the acidity rating, the darker the oil and the stronger the flavour. *'Extra virgen'* oil is around 1 per cent of acidity and is by far the most expensive; *'puro'* olive oil is usually a mixture of *virgen* oil and refined oil.

Now, with two such abundant natural products as olive oil and garlic always available it is only natural that the cook should use both in conjunction with each other, and in fact one of the most well loved sauces in Spain is *alioli*. This is made by crushing garlic cloves in a mortar; when they have been reduced to a fine pulp, olive oil is added drop by drop to achieve a fine emulsion – it is not easy and requires much practice, but do not be seduced into adding an egg yolk to stiffen it up or you will be making garlic mayonnaise, an entirely different sauce. The origins of this fine sauce have been ascribed to the early Roman poet Virgil, who is said to have made a similar sauce and eaten it with bread as an appetiser. Even today, many will vouch that this is still the only way to eat it; however, it is also an excellent accompaniment to meat, fish and game.

A plethora of Spanish cookbooks and regional recipe books have been produced in the last ten years, written in both English and Spanish. Television also provides a regular cooking spot to encourage the embryonic gastronome; however, to avail yourself of this tuition you must be able to follow Spanish spoken at a fair lick, for it seems that Spanish women in the kitchen chat a lot about many things other than what they are doing.

Because Spain is so vast and its regional differences so sharp, it is really necessary to revert once again to a regional approach to Spain's popular dishes, for most of them have a local attachment somewhere in their development. The costas have modified traditional cooking to a degree, and European fast food chains feed not only peckish tourists but many busy Spaniards as well; but putting that misfortune aside we shall refer once again as a starting point to the Cantabrian coastal regions with their Atlantic seaboard, green fields and mountain ranges, for here in Galicia, Asturias and the Basque country we find dishes that reflect the two main activities of the region, fishing and farming.

Galicia is a region particularly renowned for its seafood dishes, and none better in the view of many a Spaniard than 'Bogavante a la Gallega' – lobster Galician style: all the meat of the lobster is sautéed in onion and garlic, paprika and oil, then lightly casseroled in wine. Best among her soups is 'Caldo Gelleqo'; made from ham, beans, beef, potatoes and chard, it is a meal in itself, and like the Mallorquin soup is often eaten as such with hunks of fresh bread.

A little further along the coast **Asturias** produces fine

dishes from locally caught salmon, bass and trout, and none finer than 'Salmon a la Ribereña'; salmon steaks are lightly cooked in butter, then a sauce of flour, champagne and chopped ham is poured over and the dish is gently baked; served with a glass or two of the excellent local cider (*sidra*) it makes a meal to remember.

Cooking is considered a fine art throughout the whole of the Cantabrian coastal zone, but it is in the *Basque* region that you find those considered to be the finest cooks. For centuries, Basque males have prided themselves on their culinary prowess, and many top restaurants throughout Spain employ Basque chefs because of this. Their specialities include many fish and seafood dishes; for example, the unpronounceable Txangurro: a crab-meat casserole cooked in tomato sauce, onion, parsley and brandy, served in ramekin dishes with a topping of buttered breadcrumbs and grated cheese. Delicious meat dishes of local venison, hare and rabbit are renowned for their richness and flavour.

This Atlantic seaboard region is not a major wine-growing area, but light white wines are produced, and among them Ribeiros and the Basque Txacolis stand out as being fresh and drinkable.

However, to the east is Navarra and La Rioja, and this is Spain's premier wine region: Navarra is the home of fine clarets, and these accompany such dishes as 'Cochifrito a la Navarra', a dish of diced lamb sautéed and cooked in parsley, garlic, lemon juice and paprika, best served – according to many – with small new potatoes and stick beans.

As well as its many fine fish dishes, Rioja produces an interesting and flavoursome meat called 'Patatas a la Riojana': chopped potatoes are cooked in oil together with pork loin, garlic, peppers and *chorizo* (cured sausage); after brief frying the dish is left to simmer and is finally served garnished with chopped hard-boiled egg. Accompanied by a bottle of Siglo or Marquis de Riscal, this is a fitting winter meal to sustain the most hearty eater.

Catalonia, home of the one-time conquerors of southern

Europe, has enormous variety in its menus, and none is more reflective of its past than 'Canelonas a la Catalonia': pasta shells are filled with a mixture of minced chicken breast, chicken livers, pork, veal and lambs' brains, all cooked in sherry, garlic and onion. The whole dish is served with a covering of strips of ham and grated cheese. Served with a chilled bottle of Marquis de Monistrol you will find no meal more typical of a region.

To the south is **Valencia**, the home of many fine regional dishes, from its 'Anguila al all I Pebre' – a dish of baby eels stewed in saffron, garlic, toasted almonds and paprika – to the world-famous *paella*, of which there are many varieties incorporating not only seafood but also game and meat. It is here you must try the grilled fish and *cocas* – savoury tarts and pies. To the north, *Tarragona*'s traditional dish is called 'Arroz Negro': a fine dish of rice and squid, cooked in squid ink to give both colour and flavour.

Off-shore, the **Balearic Island group** provides a gastronomic treat with each island producing its own speciality. **Mallorca**'s wonderfully light 'Ensaimadas' dipped in early morning coffee will never be forgotten, neither will her excellent lobster and tomato stew, or her *tapas* favourites of 'Coca Verdura' or 'Coca Pescada', open pastry tarts filled with chopped vegetables and tiny sardines. 'Sobrasada' is a savoury pâté cured in a sausage and eaten with rough bread and mountain ham. **Ibiza** produces excellent seafood dishes like its 'Turrida de Ratjada': poached ray served with chopped almonds.

Andalucia is the region thought by many to typify Spain, but her culinary background has been subjected to much outside influence over the centuries, and she therefore produces a wider variety of dishes than any other region in Spain. Her most famous is 'Gazpacho Andaluce', the delicious cold soup made from tomatoes, garlic, onion, cucumber and oil. It is not to be confused with 'Gazpacho Manchego' which is a rich game pâté or pie; so take care when you order. The mountain hams, *serranos*, are thinly

123

sliced and added to many dishes, or eaten on rough bread slices as a *tapas*. *Estofados* stews) of ox-tail, rabbit (*conejo*) and lamb provide winter warmth in the higher regions.

A traditional dish on the coast is 'Abaja de Algeciras', a delicious seafood stew using hake, mullet, skate, tuna grouper and rape cooked in garlic, white wine and herbs. Whilst up in **Sevilla**, 'Pechuga de Pollo a la Sevilliana' is made with boned chicken breasts cooked in sherry, oil, peppers, garlic and tomato, served and garnished with stuffed olives; and in **Malaga** pork loin is cooked in Muscatel to give 'Lomo a la Malaguena'.

The arid **La Mancha** survives its blistering summers and bitter winters to provide such dishes as 'Pisto Manchego': a *ratatouille* of distinctive flavours which accompanies many varieties of lamb and game dishes and can be washed down with any of the excellent local wines.

Madrid – the meeting-point of all roads in Spain – gives us 'Chuletas de Cerda a la Madrilena': pork chops baked with herbs and garlic, delicious when served with creamed spinach and baby new potatoes.

Extramadura lies to the west with its vineyards, olive groves and chestnut forests, and produces the conventional meals of pork, kid goat, and game; however, none is more unusual than 'Aagarto', a dish prepared from lizards and parsley – admittedly not for the squeamish, but claimed to be similar to frogs' legs in taste and texture.

Old Castile is the most ancient of all the regions, and is the home of the official Spanish language Castilliano; it is mainly high plateaux and produces much of Spain's grain. Mountain ranges provide both big and small game from partridge to ibex and wild pig. It is said to be a region of roasts, and those who have eaten the suckling pig and roast lamb served with saffroned rice and side salad would certainly vouch for this.

It is impossible in a book such as this to cover the vast variety of dishes available in Spain; a few from each region have been chosen merely as tasters, and these should be found on the menus of many good restaurants anywhere in the country. And armed with one of the multitude of excellent recipe books available, you yourself will soon be producing the exciting flavours and colours that make Spanish cooking so attractive. The methods are not complicated, and it doesn't take long to prepare an excellent three-course meal that will impress your visiting guests. So if you have the time, enjoy your cooking and your eating – most of us do.

Spanish Still Wines, Sherries and Cavas
Wine
The whole of Spain and its islands provide a suitable environment for the grape vine to grow. Wines of varying standards are everywhere produced in abundance, and marketed at seemingly ridiculously low prices when compared with their French and Italian counterparts. Control of the wine industry in Spain lies with the 'Instituto de Denominaciones de Origin' (DO). The DO insignia on a bottle is equivalent to the French 'Appellation Contrôllée' (AC), although standards are not so stringently applied as with the latter, and quality does vary considerably at times between regions.

Cheap regional wines from Valdepeñas, Soldepeñas and Valencia retail in Spain at under 50 pence a litre, and they are good wholesome wines suitable for daily accompaniment to meals. These table wines (*vinos de mesas*) are now marketed in one litre cartons (*briks*) as well as in litre bottles, and whilst the long-term keeping qualities of the *briks* may be doubtful, they certainly make a light package for tourists to take their allowance back in.

The principal wine-growing regions are best dealt with in order of prestige, so we will begin with La Rioja which runs along the banks of the great river Ebro through the provinces of Navarra and Longrono. By comparison with the rest of Spain, this is a temperate region and therefore a fine one in which to grow grapes; rainfall is adequate and the summer sun does not assault the land so viciously.

1. REBEIRO
2. RIOJA
3. NAVARRA
4. PENDEES
5. TARRAGONA
6. LA MANCHA
7. VALDEPEÑAS
8.
9. } VALENCIA
10. SEVILLA
11. JEREZ
12. BINISALEM

Wine growing regions

The three sub-regions are Rioja Alta, Rioja Baja and the one which produces the best wine, Rioja Alavera; however, Rioja Baja (lower Rioja) produces equally interesting wines, and its wonderful scenery makes by far the most attractive part of the region. Good years to look for are *Cosechas* (harvests) 1970, 1978, 1981, 1982, and 1984. Good labels are Marques de Riscal, Marques de Murrieta and Marques de Cacares. Both red and white Riojas are excellent but most people consider that the red (*tinto*) has the edge. The original estates were set up by the French – their vines had been plagued by fungal infection so they moved south to carry on their traditional activity. Bordeaux vintners occupied the Rioja region and the method of storing the vintage in oak barrels to mature survives to this day. Each bottle of authentic Rioja bears a small label on the back stating its authenticity and the regional district.

Catalonia to the west is another well established wine-producing region; the best wine is produced to the Penedes area west of Barcelona, and its whites are especially noted for their excellence. The Torres family of this sub-region has an important place among Spanish vintners, and produces famous wines like Vina Sol, Vina Esmerelda and the strong red Tres Torres and Gran Coronas. Tarragona, too, is noted for its blending and exporting of cheap wines – the chances are that if you drink your supermarket Spanish own brand in the UK you will have drunk the wine from here; or from the La Mancha region which has no less than four hundred wine co-operatives, whose output is drunk all over Spain and finds its way to most parts of the world. Try the wines from Valdepeñas, a town situated to the north of Cordoba; they are good, and its reds are said by many to compare with Beaujolais and furthermore retail much cheaper.

Sherry

To the south-west is the region of Jerez: its sherry is unique, and savoured by the whole world. It is really a re-inforced wine, but the complex system of production gives it a flavour like no other and its continuing popularity ensures its demand.

Sherry is never produced from a wine of single vintage; a system of stacking oak butts of different years and types, called a *solera*, is used to store the wines before final blending. The process for fine sherries basically consists of allowing a secondary fermentation to take place in loosely stopped carboys; a yeast flower (*flor*) grows over the wine surface while the fine sherry develops below. Then, according to the type of sherry being made, the *flor* will be killed off at varying stages with grape alcohol, which also fortifies the wine. The varieties are household names from the fine dry pale Tio Pepe, to Manzanilla, and then the more full-bodied Amontillado with its amber colour and distinct nutty flavour, also the dark Olorosos, both strong and soft to the palate.

Malaga to the south produces a sweet dessert wine which is often used in Spain as communion wine.

It would be impossible here to cover all the regions concerned with wine production; suffice it to say that the local *vinos de mesas* are always worth trying and are often surprisingly good and cheap. If you are lucky enough to live near a winery you will probably be able to get your supply direct in small glass carboys. You pay an initial deposit and they are changed 1:1; the cost of the wine is minimal.

Brandy

Brandy is made in many parts of Spain, but the principal areas of production are Jerez de Frontera and Penedes. The grape spirit used to produce brandy comes from all over Spain and is a way of using up surplus grape juice. On the whole, the final product is of good quality though if drunk in large quantities – as is the wont of some holidaymakers – it can have the disastrous results commensurate with drinking any large quantity of strong alcohol. The name *coñac* is sometimes used, much to the chagrin of the French. Many of the lighter Spanish brandies such as Bobadillos 103 and Torres Solera Selecta are indeed a very pleasant complement to a good meal, especially when warmed slightly in a large brandy balon which releases the delicate aromas.

Liqueurs
Various liqueurs are produced in many parts of Spain using ingredients ranging from coffee to hazelnuts as a flavouring agent, and all are highly alcoholic. The ones most drunk by the Spaniards are Anis and Marie Brizard; both of these are derived from fennel which grows abundantly all over Spain. Popular European liqueurs such as Cointreau and Drambuie are also made under licence, and are sold much more cheaply than in the UK. Cheap imitations are made of Baileys, Tia Maria and Cointreau, and all are marketed with only slightly different names – so beware!

Sparkling wines or Cavas
The Spanish have been making wines by the champagne method for a century, but the name 'cava' is the consequence of a long and bitter court battle in the sixties between the French and Spanish producers, when the court came down in favour of the French – hence Spanish champagne now being called *cava*, although it is viewed by many as equal if not superior to many French brand names. Among the top international sellers are Freixenet from San Sadurnida Noya, and Cororniu and Renee Barbier from Penedes. The southern regions do not in general produce good sparkling wines as the temperatures are too high for the cava-producing grape.

Sparkling wines (*vinos gasificados*) are merely white or rosé wines which have been carbonated. On the whole they do not rate highly, but if you want a cheap pop of the cork and a fizzy drink they will suffice. People with a more delicate constitution will find they tend to play havoc with the digestion if taken cold on an empty stomach.

Beer

Beer production is thriving in Spain, and ranges from the world-wide names of San Miguel and Skol to the lesser travelled Dorada, Aguila and Estrella. Currently the retail cost of a crate of 24 small bottles is under £3.00, and taken in moderation provides a cheap, thirst-quenching drink. Cans (*latas*) are much dearer, and retail at £7.00 for 24 – over double the cost; they do, however, contain more beer and are less vulnerable to breakage on a boat or a picnic.

With the low cost of alcoholic beverages throughout Spain one imagines there could be a commensurate problem of alcohol abuse among the Spanish. However, on the whole this does not follow; Spaniards themselves in fact drink a lot of mineral water and only a little alcohol by comparison with their British counterparts. A recent study of British settlers does show that once they are living here they do increase their alcoholic intake, particularly if they have no real interests; so please beware – the sun-over-the-yardarm gin and tonic could lead to a day of tipple before you know where you are, and with gin at only £3.00 a litre, it would be cheap, too.

The Spanish Club de Gourmets publishes three excellent guides to eating and drinking in Spain, though as yet it is unfortunately only written in Spanish. Their monthly magazine *Gourmentour* is full of details on regional dishes and places to eat, and their annual practical guide to Spanish wines (*Guida Practica de los vinos de España*) has two indexes, one on *bodegas* and one containing over 2,800 wines. This year they gave special awards based on their readership, firstly to Miguel Torres of Vilafranca del Penedes, which was also voted bodega of the year; also the Blanc en Noir of Marques de Monistrol was voted best white wine of the year, with Artadi '87 of Cosecheros Alaveses getting the award for the best young red.

They are also about to produce their second edition of the *Practical Guide to Spanish Cheeses* which is very comprehensive in its detail of the many hundreds of cheeses produced throughout the Spanish regions.

Keeping in Touch with Home

Since Spain is such a short distance from the UK keeping in contact is easy, never more than a two-hour flight or a phone call away.

The telephone service

The telephone service in Spain (*Telefonica*) is based on a system set up by an American company over seventy years ago. It is now a public company offering a cheap but efficient service which is greatly supported by Spain's fifty million plus visitors each year, most of whom are eager to make at least one phone call home to say how their holiday is going. With this sort of extra use Telefonica has been able to embark on projects of technical developments that have left their European counterparts standing. Fibre-optics, vandal-proof booths, cheap calls all illustrate how well the company is faring. A call to the UK is a simple matter: all public telephones take 5, 25 and 100 peseta coins, and the cost of a three-minute call is currently about £3.00 during the day and £1.50 after ten o'clock at night.

Getting a telephone installed in your flat or villa will only present a problem if you are not the owner, so if you are renting ask the owner if he will go ahead with the installation at your expense. Currently this costs about £60.00 initially and about £6.00 a month rental which may include some free call units – the exact number varies according to the region you live in.

If the apartment or villa is your own, you may yourself apply to Telefonica to have a phone installed. In some areas this may be done by just calling the local sales department and a representative will call. In other areas it is necessary to visit the Telefonica office armed with your passport and the deeds to your property (*escritura*). You will then sign a contract and go on the waiting list; depending on where you are living, the waiting time varies from ten days to four or more years. Telefonica staff do not generally speak English.

A tip when phoning the UK from Spain: the initial

connection is charged at a higher rate than the following minutes so make sure the other party is going to answer the phone or will be nearby when you ring; by the same token a wrongly dialled number can be equally expensive. For the UK dial 07 and wait for a different tone; then dial 44, and then the area code minus the '0' (thus London is 71 or 81 and not 071 or 081), immediately followed by the number required.

The postal service
Postal services vary considerably from one region to another, and from season to season. By comparison with the UK they are not good and most British residents keep a good supply of UK stamps to hand and send their important letters back in the care of someone returning to the UK to be posted there. The cost of a letter to Spain is that of a first-class letter in the UK, but it will take anything from six days to a month to arrive. Express letters fare a little better, costing 50 pence from Spain to the UK and slightly less the other way. But be warned: an express letter payment does not guarantee delivery, and many go astray at the Spanish end. However, certified delivery still costs only 50 pence from Spain, and does more or less guarantee it will get there. Certified letters arriving in Spain require the recipient to visit the nearest Spanish post office (*oficina de Correos*) to sign and collect the letter or parcel. Tip: take your passport, as you will have to verify who you are. Regular letters and cards from Spain to the UK cost about 23 pence; they can be deposited at the post office or in the yellow post boxes (*buzóns*) seen in towns and villages, but as there is no specific collection from these – especially in closed-down holiday resorts – the post office presents the safer bet to get your letters home.

Newspapers
Newspapers in English are produced by many of the tourist areas and major towns. They are of a good quality, tabloid form and usually contain a wealth of information

about local happenings, fiestas, the exchange rate, weather and the ever-important, small advertisement section where everything from a canary to a car or villa will be advertised. The world news is usually from Reuters or the Press Association and a day old.

All the English daily and weekend papers are flown out to Spain. They can be bought on the day of publication in high season in most resorts, and a day later elsewhere. They cost a lot more than the UK price: the *Daily Telegraph* is £1.00, the *Daily Mail* 80 pence and the *Sunday Telegraph* £2.00. All the UK glossy magazines cost about treble their UK price.

Radio

Radio broadcasts are made in English in most resort areas; they do contain short news items, but they mainly follow the form of BBC Radio 2 with the emphasis on music and chat. The BBC World Service broadcasts the news on the hour, and intersperses the daily broadcasting time with Radio 4-style programmes of current affairs and general interest. The frequencies best heard in Spain are as follows:

between 0800 and 1915	19 metres	15.070MHz
between 1815 and 0100	31 metres	9.410MHz

all in the shortwave band. Many locally produced English language papers will give you a programme guide for the BBC World Service.

Television

Television viewing is very popular in Spain and the technical quality is excellent. However, do not expect to bring your television from the UK and get it to work right away – it will receive a picture, but no sound. The local television shop can rectify this for about £10.00, but you would do better to buy a new set in Spain; prices are only slightly dearer than in the UK and a Spanish guarantee means trouble-free viewing should anything go wrong.

There are three main channels: TVE 1, 2 and 3, and there is a plethora of chat shows, game shows, football, basketball and bullfighting, and occasionally very good wildlife and history programmes. All programmes are broadcast in Spanish or the regional language, and in certain areas dual broadcasting is now being tried whereby a simple modification to your television or video will allow you to hear the programme or the film in the original soundtrack. So far it is being tried with *Neighbours, Dallas, Eastenders, Black Adder, Open University* and *The Equaliser*.

Satellite television opens up about ten or more channels to the viewer, many in English transmitted from the BBC, from the USA and Scandinavia. Reception for this is improving, but the cost of basic installation is well over £1,000, so for many it must wait; also, British-tuned satellite systems do not work here without considerable modification, so check before you bring one out.

Fax
Fax must also be mentioned as a means of getting urgent information back and forth from the UK. Currently an A4 sheet costs about £3.50 to transmit and £1.00 to receive, so it is quite a viable system for that important letter or bank statement.

7

Work or Retirement in Spain

Getting Work

First a word of warning. Do not think for one moment that because of the pleasant climate and the extended holiday season with its influx of potential customers that working in Spain can produce a more lucrative or laid-back way of life than in England; it certainly cannot. Spain has some of the highest unemployment figures in Europe, and there is almost no social security support for the unemployed – the little they do get stops altogether after six months. The competition for jobs is therefore high, especially as many working in the service industries have at least two jobs going at any one time both to compensate for the poor pay, and to allow for the possibility of one closing or giving them the sack; nor are employment rights as well established in Spain as they are in the UK, although things are improving gradually. As a foreigner you will have next to no chance of getting a work permit if upon application you put waiter, barman, shop assistant, taxi driver, or any other type of driver for that matter, for these are jobs that many Spaniards are queuing up for; so you will have a slim chance of being taken on legally, and legally is the operative word.

During your holidays in Spain you are bound to have met young English folk who appear to be enjoying full employment, selling time-share apartments, disco tickets, working in bars and generally odd-jobbing around. However, the majority of them are illegal, and should they get caught they will be deported immediately and their employer – if he can be traced – will be fined in excess of £2,000. Spain is tightening up, so go through the proper procedures, long-winded though they are, and at least gain peace of mind, for once deported you may not be able to enter Spain again for at least twenty-four months, and that can present many problems if you own a property there.

If you are contemplating working for someone else in Spain, first make sure that the person can legally employ you. In many regions, businesses run by foreigners that have established a limited company (SA) may only employ Spanish nationals; so check first, and if the company is not SA then get them to send you a work contract approved by the Spanish Ministry of Labour. Take this to your nearest Spanish Consulate together with your passport with minimum validity of 180 days, three passport-sized photos and three fully completed visa application forms. The following should also be taken for legalisation, as they will be required by the local authorities in Spain: details of the company or business employing you, a job description, and photocopies of the first five pages of your passport.

If you are taking furniture or household effects be sure of the procedure for exporting these (see pp43–4) before you make your visit to the Spanish Consulate. The cost of the visa provided and the cost to legalise your documents is currently £22.50, to be paid in *postal orders*. As a general rule the documents will be ready for your collection the following day.

On arrival in Spain you may well find yourself in the hands of a company solicitor who will field you through the maze of procedures; however, should there be no such luxury, you will also require a medical certificate saying you are fit to work, signed by an authorised Spanish doctor; and a certificate of proof that your company is registered with the Spanish Social Security – this goes together with your work contract to the local police headquarters. A warning: queues there will be long, and you will need an interpreter if you do not speak Spanish. This done, you will then have to wait up to six months to get your combined work permit and *residencia*, so have with you enough money to live on, or go back to the UK in the interim. DO NOT WORK

IN SPAIN without the necessary permit, no matter what anyone may tell you, or the sanctions mentioned above will be swiftly applied. It is not possible to say how soon your permit will be available; however, as soon as it is, ensure that your social security payments are made on the last day of each month.

A professional person suffers similar constraints: if you are a dentist, doctor, vet, psychologist, engineer, lawyer, scientist or architect you will be required to take a Spanish examination in your subject and gain affiliation to the Spanish college of that discipline. Even then this does not guarantee that you will be allowed to practise, as you will inevitably be competing against Spaniards with similar qualifications.

On 25 September 1978 the convention abolishing the legalisation of certain foreign documents (The Hague, 5 October 1961) came into force between the UK and Spain. It did not, however, apply to the professional qualifications received from universities, colleges, hospitals and other examining bodies; therefore all professional qualifications, from ordinary diplomas in skills to first class Honours degrees, should be formally presented to the Foreign Office in London (Legalisation Department, Clive House, Petty France, SW1.) The procedure for this is as follows: first, take your certificate to a solicitor who has known you for a while; he will attach a sworn statement stating that the certificate is yours, and then seal it; he will then forward it to the Foreign Office who charge £3.00 per certificate. These documents will then have full validity in Spain should you present them to obtain a work permit.

Setting Up a Business
As a general rule, those EC citizens wishing to establish a business in Spain were free to do so from 1 January 1986. However, like all things in Spain this is not necessarily so easy for in order to work – even in your own business – you must first obtain a work permit; even at the outset you would therefore be well advised to seek the services

of a lawyer (*gestor*), and if possible a business consultant who is well versed with the running of foreign businesses in Spain. Even as an EC citizen you will find that it is not quite as straightforward to get things started as it would be if you were a Spanish citizen doing the same thing. The rule is always: get advice, do a lot of market research, and get authentic confirmation that your project will be approved, before you invest or part with even a peseta. Many people come to Spain with grand ideas which by all accounts should work out well, given the opportunity. But there have also been cases where a proposed business project has been submitted and turned down; followed shortly by another with – miraculously! – exactly the self-same idea and what do you think! – it has been approved.

Taxes are complex, and the documentation involved will require the services of a professional unless you are particularly fluent in Spanish and tax jargon. VAT (Spanish IVA) is also complex and needs a professional to sort through the paper-work, so take the cost of this service into account, too. Business life is not half as laid back as it is in the UK, and there are many rules – for instance, you may not advertise in any paper, either for work or offering a service, without the sanction of the local Ministry of Labour who will want to see all your papers before giving approval. If your business does not turn over – *in pesetas* – a figure which the tax authorities deem viable enough to sustain you, they may remove your work permit. From the Spanish point of view, this is a precaution against someone setting up a dummy business and earning money doing something which has not been approved, or for which they have no work permit.

All this sounds awful, doesn't it? But one hears so many sad stories of ventures failing and people suddenly having to go back to the UK, when in most instances failure could have been avoided had they sought genuine advice, and not listened to the local experts who give free advice every day in bars and other social centres where the idle like to gather.

On a more positive note, approval is likely to be given for any reasonable business which employs Spaniards and brings money into Spain, especially if it is likely to generate similar spin-offs. Remember that a lot of business premises in Spain are leased, which is why you see more advertisements for business 'transfer': as in the UK, the purchaser takes over the lease on a down payment, together with the cost of the fixtures and fittings, and continues to pay the rent until the lease expires. This is particularly applicable to bars and restaurants in resort areas, though rents here are at times prohibitive and ensure that the only real winner will be the property owner.

Job Opportunities

A person who is a teacher by profession, is fluent in Spanish, and holds a 'Teaching English as a Foreign Language' (TEFL) qualification, is more or less guaranteed work in any part of Spain or its islands. That profession apart, you should consider the region where your skills or services will most probably be needed.

At first you will almost certainly choose an area where there are other British people around, either in residence or holidaying or working; there is then bound to be some administrative machinery set up which would cope with your problems – perhaps a lawyer or a business consultant, both of whom speak some English or are indeed English themselves.

Thus in the resorts one sees the following British-owned: bar, car hire, restaurant, plumber, electrician, removals, second-hand goods etc. It is a safe place to start, you are surrounded by other British people of similar outlook, and provided you are not setting up next door and in opposition you will on the whole find a 'wartime'-like spirit of helpfulness among them. All the Mediterranean costas have their British communities, and those that are making a successful living have learned that in order to compete with the Spanish you have to work just as hard and as long as they do, and that nothing just happens without effort.

Once you are in business, either for yourself or when working for someone else, do keep accurate financial records. Your bank will take over your social security payments – all you have to do is take the book of payment slips to them and they will do the rest. Social security payments are very high in Spain; currently a self-employed person pays £76.00 monthly and the employer of a worker pays up to about £120 monthly, but the worker's contribution is minimal. However, for this payment the contributor enjoys the full use of the state National Health Service system for himself and his family, and provided he has made arrangements before leaving the UK, his Spanish social security contributions can be credited towards his UK entitlement for retirement pension.

Current Work and Business Prospects

There are very many different ways in which British people can earn a living in Spain. In these days of equal job opportunities it would be impossible to lay down any particular rules to differentiate between those jobs which are done exclusively by men and those done by women, except perhaps that a woman is more likely to be employed as an au pair, a housekeeper, nanny or governess, and a man as a builder, plumber or carpenter, electrician or handyman. Furthermore, work opportunity is far greater for British people along the holiday costas where the English language is universally spoken, and a business run by a British person is more likely to succeed, and will be more easily run if it is situated in a resort area.

Let us deal with business first: it must be stressed that any business will always have the greater advantage if one of the owners speaks Spanish well. So many people try to manage by using business agencies and consultants, only to find their profits are being milked away in fees and charges for tasks which, but for the language barrier, they could without doubt do for themselves. Also, the Spanish authorities will always consider more favourably a business which will generate money and jobs for Spain. So, if your business attracts foreign money and gives jobs to Spaniards, it must have a good chance of success.

Among the current businesses doing well are yacht chandlers, and language schools; car, motor cycle and bicycle hire; sailing, and water-ski schools; flat-letting agencies and business consultancies, together with property developers and time-share agents. Among those doing badly are many bars, restaurants, gift shops and novelty shops; jewellers, hairdressers, secondhand shops and estate agencies; and finally, nursing homes. Now, this does not mean that all the former are doing well or that all the latter are packing up and going home: far from it – in fact many bars run by British people are making a fortune, and many vehicle hire firms are going broke.

So why do some businesses succeed when others fail? In a word, it is down to market research and the perseverance of the individual. A bar in a back street in Torremolinos may attract a very pleasant clientele during high summer, when the front line bars are full to bursting point with all the noise and clamour of this resort. But in the high season that landlord must make enough to keep him through the winter, unless he is very lucky and has built up a good residents' trade to support him during the lean times. Rates, rent, lighting all have to be paid for, and many of those people who race out to buy the bar they enjoyed visiting during their summer holidays very soon find that from the end of October to the beginning of April it is practically deserted.

Gift shops and novelty shops, unless they are perfectly sited for year-round trade, suffer badly from seasonal decline. Regrettably they also suffer a lot of pilfering when, at the height of the season, the pavements are crowded and eyes cannot be everywhere. Break-ins are frequent, and if a shop sells expensive items insurance premiums are

141

high unless a full alarm system is fitted. The Spanish government's most recent requirement is that businesses are properly equipped with toilet and washing facilities. This doesn't sound much, but it may be quite a burden – when a snack bar or café has to be plumbed in from square one it can be expensive when added to the in-going premium.

The property letting business is another area where many have caught a financial cold recently. Down the years it has been viable to buy two or three studios or small flats, and make a living from letting them out throughout the year. A studio can bring in £100 a week in high summer and about £30 to £50 in the winter on a long let. However, heretofore the earnings from these little enterprises were not declared: now, all property that is let must be registered at the local municipality and tax paid, and the earnings must be audited and another tax paid to *hacienda* (inland revenue). This means a considerable drop in earnings and a lot of administration for the owners, many of whom are now selling up and getting out.

There are other areas of business still to be developed which are worth considering, but almost without exception they must be sited in or near a tourist region where the ever-flowing numbers of people will provide the clientele. For example, golf-driving ranges do not need the vast area of land that is taken up by golf courses; they are few and far between and those attached to golf courses charge heavy extra premiums to non-members using their facilities. One known to the author makes a standing entry charge of £7.00 and £3.00 for a bucket of balls, in an effort to keep casual users away – and it is always crowded.

Microlite flying and hang gliding are areas to explore; both are ideally suited to many parts of Spain and to date very few schools have been established. Horse riding schools are needed, and trekking centres could be set up to provide inclusive holidays on the lines of those in Wales and Dartmoor. Squash courts and fitness complexes could pay dividends if they were efficiently run and provided certified courses of tuition; so could RYA affiliated sailing schools and yacht training centres. Currently, certified training is simply not offered; businesses seem content just to hire out equipment and boats and rake in the money. Bowling alleys could be considered; they provide a year-round earner, yet there are few of them around.

Nor are there many secondhand furniture and bric-a-brac shops in a country where furniture prices are high and rising. Book shops and lending libraries are starting to appear in many of the winter resorts, and these also do well. However, avoid video hire – the complexities of rights and taxes have put many out of business and out of pocket. Inland, bed and breakfast holidays have not yet been developed to anywhere near their potential; if the proprietor is fluent in the language and offers guided tours of the area it will certainly fill a need for those holiday-makers who want to know a bit more about Spain and prefer to avoid the costas.

Flat- and villa-minding can be a very pleasant way for a semi-retired couple to spend the winter, especially if they have an interest in gardening, general DIY and animals – many people prefer to leave their cats and dogs in their own environment than put them in kennels. This is another potentially profitable area: there are not many good catteries and kennels to be found in Spain; however, those that are established charge from £2.50 a day for a cat and £4.00 plus for a dog, so there is money to be made if you have a way with animals and are sufficiently knowledgeable about them.

The universal slogan that always seems to win custom is the prefix 'British-run or British-owned'. The British customer feels safer hiring a car, depositing his cat, or having his plumbing fixed by someone he can communicate with; however, at present the British-run businesses charge more for their services than do the similar Spanish ones, and do not always give such a good service; thus it would seem that a well run, reliable British business which charges a fair price for its services would have a very good chance of success down the coast from the Costa Brava to the Costa del Sol – and there is plenty of evidence to support this statement.

All in all, it appears that those who are doing well in Spain are succeeding because their formula is hard work, good market research and an emphasis on developing good customer relations, coupled with an equal partnership with the Spanish authorities.

Working for Someone
The chance of finding a job that pays anything like a UK salary is almost nil – you must be prepared to earn less, and at the same time perhaps to do more. For example, the couriers and guides who work for travel companies are usually only employed for the season; during that time they earn about £80 a week and are provided with a uniform, but may have to share a flat with other couriers. Planes and problems arrive at all hours of the day and night, the clients are not always reasonable people – cases of verbal and physical abuse are not infrequent – and the only perk, as such, is a commission on the excursions they sell (usually about 10 per cent). Some holiday firms offer free flights at the end of the season and discount off some package holidays, some offer meals in their own hotels; but on the whole it is a pretty hard and underpaid existence without much job satisfaction either.

Qualified nurses are being paid about £3.00 an hour for day work and £4.00 for night duty so there is unlikely to be a rush to work in the costa nursing homes. However, private nursing can be quite lucrative and rewarding – many elderly people want to retain their independence, and private nursing helps out through difficult times. A nurse doing this work must obtain an autonomous work permit (costs about £300) and pay £75 a month social security; so be sure of your income before you start. And teachers, beware – especially those who have TEFL certification, as teachers are being exploited by small, badly run English language schools. Currently some are offering only £15 to £20 for an eight-hour teaching day and the work is boring and repetitive, like a sausage factory churning out sausages. The more enterprising teachers are setting up their own mini-schools and giving private tuition, but before they even start the autonomous permit must be obtained and social security payments made – so be sure of your income before you start!

The marinas offer a wide range of jobs both in and out of season. If you are a qualified Master you can earn up to £50,000 a year all found. More realistically, yacht-minding, servicing, crewing, or delivery all provide satisfactory incomes, usually with accommodation on board. The status of people doing this work is rather flexible and so they do not always pay taxes. However, if you do take a job on a yacht, get yourself some medical insurance or ensure that the owner has you covered on his policy.

Golf and tennis professionals make a comfortable income; so do the few doctors, vets, dentists and accountants who have become affiliated to the Spanish regulating bodies for these disciplines.

Many building workers, carpenters, plumbers and electricians have come out to join the growing number of British builders, all of them setting up shop in Spain so as to be one step ahead of the 1992/93 regulations coming into force.

A sports coach will always find work in a hotel or a sports complex, and physiotherapists, acupuncturists, homoeopaths, and relaxation therapists regularly advertise their services in the English language papers – though whether or not they are legal or even qualified, one cannot say.

Journalism, writing, and art in all its forms is earning a reasonable living for many. There are the English language papers to which you could contribute, and English language glossy magazines have started to appear, full of general chat about life on the costas; so if writing or art is your forte, you have openings here.

Interior decorators and designers pander to the fads of the rich in their apartments and villas, so if you have a flair for this some market research will reveal the possibilities. Certainly painters and decorators always get work – though not always legally.

Finally, a word of warning to young people, because it appears that they are the most vulnerable to exploitation. Time-share blocks, discos and other enterprises that require street touts almost always employ young people – the pay is strictly by commission and invariably illegal. The trap falls in the off-season, and many of these youngsters band together in cheap holiday apartments with little or no income. Drugs are prevalent here in Spain and it is the young people who use them. The street workers are almost always involved either directly or indirectly with the dealers, and this leads to considerable exposure to both petty and major crime – the Spanish police are currently waging a war against both. So the policy should always be to *avoid* street work of *any* sort: it is fraught with danger from both physical and moral abuse. One group which was recently apprehended was reminiscent of Fagin's organisation in *Oliver Twist*; at their rented flat the police found drugs, credit cards, beach bags, TVs and videos, jewellery, passports and a host of other items – all stolen. So beware!

The Spouse
There is no rule that makes it mandatory for the spouse of someone working or living in Spain to become resident, and many partners choose to retain tourist status with all the benefits that accompany that condition. They can buy and run a car on tourist plates thus saving a third of its purchase price, they can hold both foreign currency deposit and current accounts, and they are not liable to Spanish social security contributions. However, if they tot up more than 180 days in Spain they will be liable to Spanish income and wealth tax, and the to-ing and fro-ing to keep their tourist status can cost a lot in travel and may raise eyebrows if they keep requesting leaving and entry

stamps at the border control or airport to substantiate their compliance with the 90-day rule.

Retirement in Spain
The special position of the UK pensioner
Since entering the EC, pensioners from the UK have been afforded special rights with regard to their taking up residence in Spain. The key word here is residence, because if they are only staying for part of the time in Spain and part of the time in the UK then the special entitlements do not apply; and if they do not overstay their permitted 180 days continuous period in Spain, they can continue life with all the benefits of being a tourist, can hold foreign currency accounts, and drive cars on tourist plates. However, to take up permanent residence in Spain for the purpose of retirement the following routine should prove useful, and ensure that the pensioner takes the smooth path to *residencia* and gets all that he or she is entitled to.

Before leaving the UK
You must first decide how you wish to receive your pension in Spain, and then make provision to see that it will be available for you to draw when you need it. The safest way is to get it paid into a UK bank account (current) and cash sterling cheques in your Spanish bank as you need the money. You may ask 'Why not get the money paid directly into a Spanish bank?': on the grounds of cost alone this is impractical, as credit transfers from the UK to Spain are expensive and do not always arrive on time, and at worst fly off into some form of time-warp and take a lot of tracking down. If you have a good bank in Spain, the price of encashing a UK cheque should amount to little more than the currency conversion rate.

Spanish authorities will require evidence of the annual value of your pension; they will also need to know if tax has been paid, and at what rate. If you are lucky you may get your pension authority to pay your pension without deduction of tax, because if you declare it in Spain you will be taxed at a lower rate than the UK, and will not have to pay the tax until the end of the Spanish fiscal year. People in receipt of pensions from local authorities, do not, however, seem to be successful in getting their pensions paid gross, whereas those paid from central government sources do. Spanish authorities are only interested in the fact that taxes have or have not been paid and that the residue is sufficient for the pensioner to live on. The figure accepted currently is about £250 a month, and rising; if your pension comes to less than this the Spanish authorities fear that you may engage in some form of illegal working activity to augment it, that's all. You may supplement your pension at any time by spending capital, but keep the exchange transaction receipts as evidence to support this added expenditure.

A last word on money: many pensioners use UK-based off-shore banks and have their pensions paid direct to them. They earn interest of up to 11 per cent on a 28-day account, and they provide a cheque book for drawing money in Spain when it is needed. The interest is paid without deduction of UK tax, and can be declared annually at their preferential rate if desired.

A visit to the Spanish Consulate in the UK is next on the agenda, armed with your UK passport which must be valid for at least 180 days, also three passport-sized photographs and three fully completed visa application forms (acquired by post previously). Normally your visa will be ready for your collection on the next working day, and the consulate may even forward the visa to you if you provide a large stamped and addressed envelope. The cost of this visa is currently £22.50 to be paid in *postal orders* at the time, so go prepared.

If you are taking personal effects with you to Spain check the requirements regarding export (see pp43–4) and take all the relevant forms with you to the consulate; everything can then be dealt with at the same time.

So far so good: for importing cats and dogs see p45 and

if you are taking your UK-purchased vehicle, see p46.

Health care
Since joining the EC Spain has had a reciprocal health cover agreement with its European partners. Retired persons should obtain form E121 from the DHSS before leaving the UK, and a letter briefly stating that they intend taking up residence in Spain should be addressed to: DHSS, Overseas Branch, Central Office, Longbenton, Newcastle-upon-Tyne, NE98 1YX.

On arrival in Spain, take the duly completed E121 form to your local Spanish Social Security offices (Instituto Nacional de la Seguridad Social): you will be issued with a book of vouchers, a list of doctors whom you may consult, and hospital services you may use. You need have no fears concerning the Spanish social security system as it is very good; see p79 on health care and then decide whether or not you will want to take out private medical insurance.

If you are receiving an invalidity pension or social security financial support grant, please check thoroughly with them the details regarding your position, and well before you leave the UK. There are reciprocal arrangements regarding invalidity rights, but they must be confirmed before your departure.

On arrival in Spain
To obtain your *residencia* take the documents you have obtained from the Spanish Consulate in the UK to a reliable solicitor (*gestor*), or to an agent who advertises the service of obtaining *residencias* and work permits. It may take ages for your *residencia* to come through – one sometimes hears stories of waits of six to eight months – but don't worry; once you have evidence that your application is being made, you can sit back and relax until you are sent for. The cost of this service should not far exceed £25.00. Eventually you will be summoned to the local police headquarters where your right index finger-print will be taken and you will be issued with your *residencia*

card. The expiry date can usually be found in the bottom left-hand corner.

Please remember that once you become a resident your position changes with regard to banking and car ownership – see pp47–9.

The senior citizen in Spain

As a senior citizen you will be joining a fast-growing population of older people who are moving south first to get away from the rigours of the northern European winters, and also from increasing violence and the rising cost of living.

Retirement in Spain can mean two distinctly differing ways of life, depending on the wont of the pensioner. If he has worked hard all his life and feels that now is the time for a good rest, Spain provides the ideal environment in which to flop and do little more than take in the sun and food.

For the slightly more active, however, Spain provides much more. There are clubs and groups springing up everywhere to fulfil an ever-growing range of interests, and lending and exchange libraries provide all the books you never got around to reading in your working life. Diverse interests which include meditation through yoga, Japanese painting, Spanish language lessons and cooking are being catered for, either within the community or by the English-speaking schools or clubs.

The church is particularly active with rotas of people making hospital and home visits to those who are not well, running thrift shops, organising outings and generally making themselves useful in the community.

Animal protectionists will be glad to know that in a land that countenances bull fighting there is nonetheless a strong sense of responsibility towards other animals. Dispensaries and cats' and dogs' homes are of a high standard, but all need more funds to keep running efficiently, and many pensioners find an almost full-time job organising schemes to augment this constant need for cash.

If during your retirement you have planned to extend your learning even further, the Open University does have some programmes transmitted in dual language (see pp133–4, Television) and work units can be posted to and from the UK.

Golf, if that is your sport, is very popular amongst retired people, with 365 warm golfing days a year in mid- and southern Spain; it provides good exercise and value for money, even if the membership fees *are* expensive. One senior citizen was heard to rationalise his high subscriptions thus: 'Well, if I play every other day, after six months I will be paying about £2.00 a round'. Good luck to him, and he'll certainly be fit!

To those of you who are not so well, Spain has such an acceptable climate that it can really enhance the quality of life. To look out and see blue skies, to feel the warm breeze, and to find, all the year round, fresh and reasonably priced food which will make the pension go that little bit further – all this must make any condition more bearable. Arthritis sufferers in particular find great relief in the warm weather, and the benefits of sea-bathing are renowned. The index gives a list of spas and health farms for those who are sufficiently well off to enjoy their alleged benefits; but for those who cannot meet their cost, the sun, the wine and the food alone will, without doubt, have an equally beneficial effect.

So if you are of a mind, try Spain.

8

Your Personal Finances in Spain

Banking
This is possibly one of the most important sections in the book if you are contemplating a stay of more than six months.

Ten or fifteen years ago Spanish banks suffered a lot of adverse publicity due to their seemingly out-of-the-blue insolvencies. There were too many banks chasing too little money, and like stockbrokers in bad times, many banks were liquidated. However, nowadays Spain has a generally efficient, computerised banking system which serves the resident well. As the EC takes its grip many foreign banks are endeavouring to become established; one particular High Street bank has branches in most major cities. It gives a service in English, which means the documentation and correspondence are all in English, although many consider the prohibitive charges far outweigh the usefulness of the service it provides. However, the more cautious non-Spanish speaking resident may well prefer to seek its services, valuing the peace of mind given above the cost. The procedure for opening an account, and the type of accounts that may be held, applies to all banks in Spain be they Spanish or foreign, so the information that follows holds good for all.

Opening a bank account in Spain varies little from opening an account in any other country. Some banks require references, others only require a substantial deposit of currency; what matters most is the type of account you may open, and the conditions that control your holding of that account. The types of account are:

1 A basic account in pesetas

2 A foreigner's convertible peseta account
3 A foreigner's account in a foreign currency
4 A deposit account in foreign currency

Each of the above has different restrictions which in turn depend upon the status of the person holding them.

Thus, taken in order: a basic current account in pesetas may be held by anyone, whether he is a visitor or a resident. This gives the resident, in addition to a cheque book, the chance to obtain a cheque guarantee card and a visa card should he so desire.

A convertible peseta account may only be held by a non-resident, and as soon as he acquires residency (*residencia*) he must immediately relinquish this account and transfer the balance into an ordinary peseta account, or convert it back into sterling and send it out of Spain. Only convertible pesetas may be converted back into their original currency, and only whilst the holder is non-resident. As a matter of interest, all monies that have passed through a convertible peseta account can be cashed back into sterling should the resident ever decide to leave Spain permanently, so it is advisable to keep a record of cheque stubs and bank certificates (mentioned below) up to the date of obtaining final residence.

Foreign currency accounts (*cuenta extranjera*) are useful for the non-resident to hold money in whilst weathering out a period of poor exchange rate, or for paying bills in that currency should this be necessary. All foreign currency accounts have to be closed on obtaining residence, and the balance either converted into pesetas or sent out of Spain.

Deposit accounts in sterling offer very favourable rates to the non-resident, and of course have the added advantage of allowing gross payment without the deduction of any taxes. The minimum investment period is one month and the maximum is twelve months. Special interest rates are given for amounts over £20,000.

The advantages of having a Spanish bank account

153

stretch beyond the mere convenience of having money
safely on hand, so it is worthwhile examining the types
of service banks offer and the reliability with which they
execute them.

Spanish banking hours vary from summer to winter
months. In summer they generally open from 9am to
2pm Monday to Friday. In winter they open from 9.30am
to 1.30pm Monday to Friday, and 9.30am to noon on
Saturdays. Beware the *fiesta*; there are many, and banks
usually close for them.

On opening an account you will be issued with the
appropriate cheque book or books, and it is wise to
remember that the laws on the presentation of, and
payment by, personal cheques are different from our own
laws. For example, cheques are valid for six months only,
and after that time have no value. Post-dated cheques
can be presented ahead of their date and payment will be
made if funds are there, so take care. Even if the funds in
an account are insufficient, a bank must nonetheless pay
out all the money there is to the presenter of the cheque,
in part payment. Also, there is an established procedure
which can be set into action against anyone offering
worthless cheques, so make sure your account always has
sufficient funds to cover any cheques you sign, and don't
post-date any.

A word of warning about making cheques payable to
the bearer (*el portador*): you may be asked to give such
a cheque to a person who has no bank account through
which to cash it – it is equivalent to a UK cheque made out
to 'cash', but there the similarity ends. A bearer cheque is
regarded as currency and may keep changing hands up to
its six months of validity thus causing confusion in your
account. So only give bearer cheques to those whom you
know will present them right away – or better still, don't
issue them at all but pay cash.

Other services offered by Spanish banks include those of
paying bills by standing order, which is highly convenient
if you wish to avoid long queues in the electricity offices,

Telefonica, town hall etc. For the employed, banks will pay social security payments and private medical insurance premiums, as well as run special accounts for those who are in a business of their own. Overdrafts, business loans and mortgages are also available, but the interest rates charged are high and there are also various setting--up fees which make short-term loans non-viable. Mortgages are usually given over a period of ten to fifteen years, though the payments required are altered with the changes in the interest rate, and without consultation, so be careful. Loans will not normally be entertained except for house and land purchase unless the borrower is resident.

Two important things to remember about Spanish banking are that statements are normally sent only on request, and that all business correspondence is in Spanish. In larger cities and resort areas you will find banking staff who speak English, but any correspondence will be in Spanish, as will cheques and statements.

Spanish Tax Liabilities

For the purposes of taxation, you are considered to be a resident if you live in Spain for more than 182 days per year, and as such you have to pay taxes on your *world* income.

The *Impeustos Sobre la Renta de las Personas Fiscas* (Personal Income Tax) is a direct, progressive and a personal tax. It involves direct assessment of the total net income that a person or family receives from all sources, and is demanded progressively according to a scale laid down by Hacienda (the Spanish tax authority). Account is also taken of the individual circumstances of the family unit and allowances are made accordingly, thereby arriving at a final tax liability for the whole family for the year.

If your gross family income does not exceed 500,000 pesetas per annum you are not obliged to make a declaration; if however, it exceeds this amount, from whatever source, you must make a declaration.

You should declare all of the following: salary from employment or self-employment and any pensions paid to you. Income from dividends, bank interest, annuities etc, rental income from any property let by you. Income from business activities or professional services given by you. Increase or decrease in the capital value of your assets. However, the following are exempt: unemployment benefits, indemnity payments or any lottery winnings.

Double taxation relief
(For relevant information, see IR16 publication obtained from any tax office in the UK.)

Briefly, pensions are paid with tax deducted at source in the UK and this tax can be offset against Spanish tax liability. If you have decided to stay more than the statutory 182 days, it is worth writing to your UK tax authority saying that you would like to receive your income (from whatever sources) intact, without tax deduction. Forms will then be sent to you to complete and forward to Hacienda, who will then contact your UK tax authority under the reciprocal agreement. Replies can take up to six months, so write as soon as you decide.

Tax deductible allowances in Spain
These allowances include: social security contributions either paid by you if self-employed, or shared by you (if you are a salaried person) and your employer, plus a further 2 per cent of your gross salary (also allowed if your UK pension is declared as a source of income). All business and personal expenses related to work – supporting documents are needed, of course. Also expenses relating to any rental incomes – repairs, agents' fees etc. Marriage allowance of 21,000 pesetas plus 17,000 pesetas if there is more than one member of the family with an earned or unearned income.

Child allowance　　　　　　　16,000 pesetas

Life insurance   15 per cent premium

Health insurance   15 per cent premium

Special allowances are available on local government investments.

Losses can be brought forward from the previous year. There is a deadline for submission of declaration. In Spain the tax year is the same as the calendar year, and the declaration for the previous year must be sent to the province tax authority between 1 May and 20 June. If you are late with your declaration you can expect a fine and a surcharge, so get your forms in on time.

In many towns there are reliable accountants who will, for a fee, complete your declaration for you, though it is always worth knowing what they are doing for their money.

Further information on the matter of reciprocal fiscal arrangements between the UK and Spain can be obtained by writing to: The Inspector of Foreign Dividends, Lynwood Road, Thames Ditton, Surrey KT7 0DP.

Community Charges

Where a property is connected to another group of properties, as in a block of flats, or a private housing estate, the owners are obliged by law to set up and maintain a so-called 'community of owners', with an elected president and an administrator; the latter may be taken from outside the community, and in fact there are agencies now which supply professional administrators who specialise in the running of large blocks and complexes. The administrators of these blocks of flats (*edificios*), property developments (*urbanisacións*) and holiday complexes will levy community charges: these are the costs levied to owners for the efficient running of all the amenities not paid for or covered by urban taxes.

Property owners have to pay these expenses by law, and they must all attend their annual general meeting to discuss these affairs, and to elect a president and committee members. These meetings are usually fairly lively, when everything that has been building up over the previous twelve months is brought out and aired.

Items usually covered by the community charges are as follows: swimming-pool upkeep, the lighting of passages and grounds, gardens and gardeners, porter's salary, lifts, cleaning and painting, television aerials and satellite dishes, water supply, electric transformers, rubbish disposal, road upkeep etc. The cost rather depends on the style in which you live; for example, a luxury penthouse overlooking a marina with a pool, porters, cleaners and a gardener may require you to pay up to £1,500 annually – whereas for a lowly block of four flats with only exterior decoration and passage lights to cover, you may have to pay £20 a year. The rule is, you pay for what you get, so when viewing the property ask what the community charges are, and when they are due. Most banks will take over these payments if requested to do so.

A word of warning on community charges: old, run-down blocks of flats are notorious for having their community charges suddenly increased; these are often levied to pay for such items as a new lift system to replace the old one which has failed to pass the safety test, or for re-tiling the pool, or even for re-wiring the whole building – so do take care, as the bargain flat may cost more than you expect when things start to go wrong.

A community that doesn't pay its way because its members fail to meet the charges for services rendered from outside the community – such as waste disposal, electricity and water – could well find that the administration is taken over by the government department which has been set up for this very purpose. In this case, a government administrator is appointed to run the block or complex and whilst the owners do have a voice through the annual and extraordinary meetings in which they can air their views, they will find they have no say in the choice of contractors for work, and that it will be virtually impossible to have work delayed, to give the community time to save up for the job to be done. So all in all, the cost of living in a property where the government has taken over will be considerably higher, and it also follows that would-be purchasers of such properties will be very unlikely to come along because the takeover presupposes a place of moderate reputation anyway. So the rule is: don't buy a government-run property unless you think it is an absolute bargain, and unless you intend staying there for a long time.

Local Rates

As in the UK, local government is based in the town hall and provides a variety of services, all of which require funding either from central government or from individual property owners in that district. Municipal taxes (*Contribucion Territorial Urbana* if you live in a built-up area, and *Contribucion Territorial Rustica* if you live in the country) are the rates you pay that contribute to the following: service and administration, education, sanitary services, social assistance, community substructure, cultural services, sports services, etc. The list is endless, but in Spain with its growing wealth, demands are constantly being made for better roads, lighting, rubbish collection, sports facilities, libraries and children's play areas.

In the wealthier costa regions these amenities are being funded by hoteliers, by owners who let their property, and by all the other businesses that pay contributions proportionate to their share of the holiday boom. For this they get clean streets, good lighting, clean beaches, efficient policing, and help and assistance when new projects are being planned. The individual private property owner tends to pay less in these regions because he is so well subsidised. As in the UK, the owner of a small country property will pay very little because his share of the cake is proportionately smaller.

Generally, rates are based upon the square metreage of the property that has been built upon: currently, this means that the owner of a three double-bedroom, two-bathroom bungalow with terraces and a modest garden in an urban area should expect to pay around £150/£200 per year; this is a whole lot less than you would pay for a similar property in the UK, and in a country area this sum would be halved. Rates are increasing year by year, but they do keep below the inflation rate.

The rate demand is usually sent out in June, and payment must be made by mid-September or a surcharge of 20 per cent will automatically be applied. Rates can be paid by the individual at the local town hall either in cash or by a banker's certified cheque. Most people pay by banker's order through the bank – it saves both time and hassle, as there are often long queues at the town hall since many people dispute their charges as a form of sport. Should you fail to pay your rates, you may well find that in addition to the surcharge your property is embargoed.

It must be said, however, that the richer councils are working feverishly to improve their civic amenities, and sports complexes with swimming pools, gymnasiums and cultural centres are popping up everywhere – each constructed to the inimitable futuristic architectural design so typical of Spain.

Making a Will in Spain

As a property owner you are advised to make out a Spanish will; British wills do stand in Spain but you will save your beneficiaries much time and money if there is a local will made out to substantiate their claim.

The procedure and wording are in much the same form as in a UK will, though do ensure that you name as your executor a Spanish solicitor who speaks English, as all the probate procedures will need his ministrations.

Inheritance tax

Inheritance laws manifest themselves in a swingeing tax which takes account not only of the value of the estate, but who inherits it. Thus a child inheriting from a parent may pay between 12 and 20 per cent, whereas a friend who has no relationship with the deceased may pay as much as from 73 to 90 per cent. So if you are getting on in years and wish to leave your Spanish property to your family, it may be worthwhile transferring the property into their name, although this transfer will still attract IVA and *plus valia*. Better still, you could consider moving and purchasing the new property in their name, as long as you were able to end your days there – the disadvantages are a possible family rift or your need to change properties; then your kin will have to be present at the buying and selling, unless of course you get power of attorney from them.

Inheritance taxes are all under review; they affect the Spanish as much as they do us – in fact more so, considering the Spanish penchant for investing every spare peseta in a house or land – so in a few years' time things may be more reasonable.

9

Travel in Spain

The cost of travel varies, widely depending on the mode of transport chosen.

Modes of Transport

Buses

Buses are frequent and cheap for short-distance travel, but they are often crowded and can be very uncomfortable especially in the hot summer weather. A few of the more wealthy authorities now have air-conditioned bus services, but replacement of existing vehicles will be a slow process. It is also uncommon to find a driver who speaks any language but Spanish, so be sure of where you want to go and where you want to get off before boarding. A good tip is to fight your way to an exit point on the bus before you near your drop-off point. Most buses are driver-only operated – passengers enter at the front and leave by one of two side exits, and there are not many seats so as to provide maximum standing room.

Taxis

Taxis are licensed locally but their tariffs are controlled. At main taxi ranks you will find a board displaying the rates to most popular destinations, and the driver will also have a rate sheet in his cab. The rule is always to fix a price before you start your journey, then there can be no argument. Supplements can be charged for airport pick-ups and excess luggage. A driver will not often exceed the number of passengers stipulated on his permit, so if you are four or more persons be prepared to take two cabs.

Trains

The train service is excellent throughout peninsular Spain and of good time-keeping reliability. RENFE (*Red National de Ferrocarrilas Espanolas*) is the large Spanish railway network. The TALGO (*Tren Articulado Ligero Goicoechea Oriol*) is a sight to behold with its silver and red livery, and its air-conditioned carriages with jet-travel facilities of reclining seats, piped music and meals. The TALGO TEE is the trans-Europe express which clocks up speeds of 112 miles (180km) an hour. The Rapido is a day-time service which, contrary to its name, is in fact slower than the TALGO TEE; the Expreso is its night-time counterpart. The Ferro Bus and Automares cover the short distance routes, and are more in line with our commuter trains.

Obviously fares are based on distance travelled and are related to the type of train service chosen, but at the time of writing they are somewhat cheaper than train fares in the UK and of course the accommodation is far superior. Day returns and weekday returns both get reductions; so do Spanish senior citizens who pay half fare, and large Spanish families who get special discounts according to their numbers. Children between the ages of four and twelve normally pay half fare.

Domestic airlines

Internal airline routes join all the main cities and the offshore islands. Iberia, Hispania and Aviaco provide regular daily flights and in some cases the fares are reduced for families and senior citizens, and for island residents. Fares are comparable if not slightly cheaper than those found on European inter-city routes.

Road travel

Trunk roads (*carrateras*) are of good construction but are rarely dual carriageway. Motorways (*autopistas*) link most major cities and are almost without exception toll roads, though charges are reasonable; you can, for instance, travel across Spain from Bilbao to Barcelona for under £25 on a very fast modern highway which has frequent well equipped rest areas. Speeds are set at a maximum of 81 miles (130km) an hour; 68 miles (110km) an hour on 'C' roads; and 56 miles (90km) an hour on other roads unless otherwise stated. The traffic police patrol all roads and strictly enforce all the laws – the motorcycle duos (*las parajes*), with their somewhat American style, will relentlessly track down all law violators. If vehicles coming towards you are flashing their lights, they are probably warning you that you are about to approach a police trap (though also see below). Such is the aura surrounding the traffic police that one rarely sees them being overtaken even when they are cruising at considerably below the permitted speed limit.

A few tips on motoring in Spain: drivers and front seat passengers must wear seat belts outside the precincts of a town. Children are not permitted in the front seats until they are of a size to wear a seat belt effectively. Three-point turns are forbidden in built-up areas; and to park facing on-coming traffic or in one-way streets is forbidden. In built-up areas you will see parking signs with '1 al 15' and '16 al 31' on opposite sides of the street: this means that for half of the month you must park on the right side, and for the other half park on the left. A driver flashing his headlights (apart from warning you of a possible police trap) is telling you that *he* is coming through a gap – this is the exact opposite of the UK use of the signal.

Ferries

Ferry services between the mainland and the islands are excellent. They are mostly operated by a firm called Trasmediterrania, who have representative offices in London called Melia Travel; the address is: Compania Trasmediterrania, Melia Travel, 12 Dover Street, London

W1X 4NS, tel 071 499 6731. They will take bookings by telex and give you your ticket before you leave the UK. A word of warning, however: the tickets issued are *not* boarding cards, and they must be exchanged at the ferry terminal at which you embark. Open tickets are also issued (*billetes abiertos*), but in high season these are not wise as the chance of picking up a spare berth is slim. Currently the fares, mile for mile, are on a par with those charged by firms operating the UK cross-channel ferry routes. A car, plus two passengers in pulman seats, can cross from Barcelona to Palma de Mallorca for £110, a journey of eight hours' duration.

Car hire
Car hire in Spain is on the whole slightly cheaper than in other Mediterranean countries, mainly because of the enormous volume of car-hire services available. Hertz and Avis dominate numerically with fleets of thousands, but in every resort street you will find at least one private agent offering a cut-price deal for three or more days' rental. For the long stay visitor a contract hire may be the answer, at around £10 a day. (For the problems concerning bringing in and using your own car for extended periods, and of purchasing a Spanish-plated car, see p48, Importing Your Car.)

No matter what means of travel you choose, you will find Spain an exciting place to explore, its wide range of climate giving a variety of flora and fauna seldom seen together in one country. Because its architecture has been influenced by various invading races, different towns sometimes give an impression of belonging to another country at first glance. Castles are now mainly run as government *Paradors* (see below) and stand proudly on their strategic sites; monasteries, refuges and ancient feudal farmhouses evoke the Spain of Don Quixote.

From Monastery to Health Farm

The choice of places to stay whilst touring is wide and varied in both price and amenity; by far the most unusual are the monasteries and retreats, where simple accommodation and meals can be had for just a few pounds a night. Take care though – some of them are for men only, and furthermore they do require a certain promptness at meal times which is quite out of character with the usual Spanish custom. Locations are often spectacular, with hilltop positions commanding grand views of the surrounding countryside. History buffs can trace the background of these establishments through ancient books and artefacts; if you are lucky you may find a monk who can speak English, and he will delight in enlightening you about the building and the 'order'. On the whole, the religious traveller will find a welcome at Mass (*misas*), whatever denomination he subscribes to, and the church in Spain is far more outward-looking than it was in the past.

Next, and of comparable antiquity, the traveller may stay at any of the state-run Paradors, of which there are a huge number. These are ancient castles, palaces, monasteries and retreats that have been carefully renovated by the government to provide high class accommodation for the discerning traveller; the standard of amenities and service is equivalent to any four- or five-star hotel and the prices charged are of the same order. However, it is not often that you get the chance to eat your dinner in a vast palatial banqueting hall surrounded by battle emblems, trophies of war and original suits of armour, so try it once if it doesn't break the bank. Be careful, though, if and when you choose, as many purpose-built Paradors are springing up in strategic places about Spain, and whilst they all offer the same high standard of service, they do somehow lack authenticity and depart from the original concept. The Central Reservation Officer for Paradors is in Madrid; also Brittany Ferries does a Parador holiday itinerary which gives a good illustration of the type of place to expect, together with current prices.

Hostels, guest-houses, pensions and inns (*fondas*) provide good, cheap accommodation; rooms are quite large in the older buildings, but don't expect fancy plumbing or air conditioning. Remember that inland Spain can be extremely hot in the summer months, and also the mosquito population is high, so choose well – look at least for a fan and mosquito netting at the window in summer, and some form of heating if you are travelling in winter.

Hotels of every standard are available in most towns, and motels are being built as demand increases from the motoring public. Standards are comparable with any European country and prices by comparison are reasonable. Food and service, however, do vary from region to region and it is advisable to book 'room only' initially, in case there happens to be a good place nearby where you might prefer to eat.

Health farms and spas are appearing now, and although they are only few in number at the time of writing, they do illustrate Spain's keen sense of supply and demand. Few television adverts are without some hint of hope to the health-conscious, and the Spanish delight in the purgatory of diet (*regimen*) which is the topic of conversation indulged by many women chatting in the local shops. Currently health farms are very expensive places to stay, but they do offer a wide range of treatment all supervised by expert therapists under the control of a doctor.

Whatever you choose – be it hostel or health farm – be assured that the atmosphere will be calm and enjoyable. I have not mentioned the costas in this section, because I have assumed that the traveller will wish to explore the real Spain away from the heavy tourist influence.

Touring itineraries are best organised according to individual preferences. However, there are some very good guide books available which cover everything from fiestas to flamenco; the Spanish Tourist Board either in Spain or in London is always ready to advise where particular needs are to be met.

Introduction to the Language
The main Spanish language is Castilliano; this is the language of commerce and industry – the main television and radio stations broadcast in it, and you are more or less guaranteed to be understood if you use it in any part of Spain.

It is a language with good firm Latin roots, and if you have studied French you will have little difficulty in following the basic grammatical structure. But whilst correct grammar is emphasised in all Spanish-run language teaching schools, many foreigners get by quite happily in totally Spanish communities with Spanish spoken almost entirely in the present tense – the local people understand everything that is said to them, which is much more important than absolute correctness. So if your mind boggles at the word grammar, never fear – you can become quite competent without it.

The delightful thing about Spain is that everywhere you look you are bombarded with Spanish words and phrases – they love advertising, and if you carry a pocket dictionary you'd be surprised how much you can learn from bill boards and the sides of buses. But first, a word on pronunciation, because it is pointless knowing the word if you can't make people understand what it is, when you say it. For instance, you may be travelling along a road in southern Spain when suddenly the road signs to your destination peter out – a not uncommon happening. Now, say you were going to Jerez, the home of sherry, and you pronounced it in English; I guarantee you would not be understood, for it is pronounced **H**ereth, with the H sounding rather throaty, like the 'ch' in the Scottish lo**ch** and the 'z' like 'th'. But never fear: I have picked a difficult example, and really if you follow the following simple guidelines you will have no trouble in pronouncing the most complex words. Remember also there are 29 letters in the Spanish alphabet.

The alphabet: the *sounds*
a, be, ce, che, de, e, efe, ge, ache, i, jota, ka, ele, elle, eme,
ene, eñe, o, pe, cu, erre, ese, te, u, uve, uve doble, equis,
y-griega, zeta.

The alphabet: the *letters*
a, b, c, ch, d, e, f, g, h, i, j, k, l, ll, m, n, ñ, o, p, q, r, s, t, u,
v, w, x, y, z.

First, the vowel-sounds are pronounced as in the following
examples:

a	sounds like the 'a' in **mat**
e	sounds like the 'e' in **entry**
i	sounds like the 'ee' in **need**
o	sounds like the 'o' in **box**
u	sounds like the 'oo' in **boot**
u	followed by **a** is like the 'a' in **wan**
u	followed by **i** or **e** is silent

The consonants are pronounced as in the following
examples:

b	and **v** sound the same, like 'b' in **bath**
c	pronunciation depends on what follows it
c	before 'i' and 'e' sounds like the 'th' in **thick**
c	before any other letter sounds like the 'c' in **cat**
ch	sounds like the 'ch' in **chap**
d	is sounded much softer than the English 'd', at the end of a word it sounds almost like the 'th' in fif**th**
f	as in English
g	before 'i' and 'e' like the 'ch' in lo**ch**
g	before any other letter sounds like the 'g' in **gap**
h	is always silent
j	sounds like the 'ch' in lo**ch**
k	as in English
l	as in English
ll	sounds like the 'll' in bata**ll**ion

m	as in English
n	as in English
ñ	sounds like 'ny' or the 'ni' in onion
p	as in English
q	always accompanied by 'u' like the 'c' in cat
r	is rolled like the Scottish 'rrr'
s	as in English, but hissed more
t	as in English
w	only found in imported words
x	sounds like the 'gs' in rags
y	same as English, but stronger
z	always like the 'th' in thick

The glossary will help you practise, but here are a few words with an English phonetic transcription to help you with pronunciation.

English	Spanish	Pronunciation
far	*lejos*	lay-hos
near	*cerca*	ther-ka
towards	*hacia*	a-thee-a
well	*bien*	bee-en
without	*sin*	seen
excuse me	*perdone*	per-do-nay
health	*salud*	saloodh
listen	*escuche*	es-koo-chay
late	*tarde*	tar-day
ready	*listo*	lees-toe
true	*verdad*	ver-dadh
sleepy	*sueño*	swayn-yo
cold	*frio*	free-o
slowly	*despacio*	days-pa-thee-o
write	*escribo*	es-kree-bo
is there	*hay*	i-ee
who	*quien*	kee-en
know	*conozco*	ko-noth-ko
go away	*marchese*	mar-chay-say
fire	*fuego*	foo-ay-go

170

peas	*guisantes*	gee-san-tays
from	*llegada*	yay-ga-dha
Barcelona	*Barcelona*	Bar-thay-lo-na
best	*mejor*	may-hor
postal order	giro postal	hee-ro pos-tal
shoes	*zapatos*	tha-pa-tos
milk	*leche*	lay-chay

10
Returning to the UK

Only a short time ago a removals man was asked how he managed to fill his vehicle for the return journey to the UK: 'Easily – there's more people going back than coming out at the moment'. It does seem rather ironical, though, to begin a final chapter with such a statement when most of the book has been trying to show the many advantages of moving *to* Spain. Why indeed do people move back?

An analysis of most of the reasons given would probably boil down to one word, homesickness. The *sangria*-sipping holiday atmosphere does not last long once you are a resident – you do have to change your way of thinking once you start trying to integrate into the Spanish way of life, and even simple things may irritate you if you are a dyed-in-the-wool Britisher. For example, you may never come to understand *mañana* – the man who is supposed to be coming to mend your washing machine arrives a day later than promised. You may have failed to learn any Spanish and find that after six months you still have to take someone with you when you go and try to sort out your bills, which always seem to be wrong. You get frustrated and so does your interpreter who will soon tire of trotting around with you.

In business, a sort of paranoia sometimes sets in; you feel that the bureaucracy is out to get you because you are a foreigner – of course it's not true, the Spanish business-man has to suffer just the same plethora of paperwork, the only advantage he has is that the forms and instructions are written in his own language. To use a modern phrase, the Spanish are much more 'laid back' about bureaucracy, the law, insurance, paying bills, keeping appointments and the like, and it is only when something disastrous happens that they are galvanised into frenetic activity. For example, a house was to be embargoed (forcibly sold off) recently because the owner hadn't paid any bills for nearly two years. The justice arrived to supervise the entry of the bailiffs when the owner suddenly produced the money to pay his debts and all the court fees. His philosophy was that he had had the use of that money for two years, so it was worth it.

I can't really see any British person taking that road from choice – but by the same token if he's in business, he may have thousands owed to him in bad debts run up by people with the attitude of the embargoed Spaniard. The point is, it's not like the UK; the pace of life is totally different, particularly in business and commerce, and many Britishers never adjust – and suddenly they want to pack up and return from whence they came, where they understand the language, can watch television in English, get regular mail, and the newspaper the day it was printed. The sun, the mild winters, the fresh produce, the cheap wine and cigarettes are all forgotten in the need to return to pastures greener. It seems that if people are going to go back for reasons other than bereavement or their company recalling them or the like, they will do so in the first two years. It appears that this is the time it takes either to adjust or to fail to adjust; once the magic two years have passed, you will have a good chance of seeing much of your allotted time through here.

Selling Your Spanish Property

As already observed (see p66, purchase procedure), the vendor does not pay for the legal work attached to a sale; the purchaser collects the bill for the whole operation, including both the solicitor's and notary's fees.

Sounds simple, doesn't it? But like all things in Spain, it isn't. Estate agents charge 5 per cent as a flat-rate commission on all sales, and it is not always possible to avoid using their services, especially if you suddenly have to return to the UK or go elsewhere and leave the sale in their hands. Avoid them if you can, or be prepared to add 5 per cent to your asking price to cover their charges.

In the UK, an estate agent will usually give a special discount to sellers who use their services only (sole agents). In Spain, 'sole agency' means that even if you manage to sell your property privately, perhaps to a friend or even a family member, the estate agent will still have a call on his percentage – so the moral is: don't sign exclusive sales rights without proper consideration.

Your deeds (*escritura*) should be lodged with your solicitor and every effort should be made to conduct the whole sale through him. Various conveyancing agencies have been established and many estate agents are qualified to conduct a sale, but to safeguard yourself you are advised to use the services of your solicitor. The laws concerning what you may do with the proceeds of a sale are quite complex, and if you were foolish enough to try and leave Spain with the proceeds of the sale without paying the taxes you owed, the consequences could be dire indeed if you were caught.

What you can take out without questions asked is the sum of the foreign currency you brought into Spain to make the purchase, plus a reasonable appreciation added for interest – this figure will be decided by the Spanish authorities. They do not automatically allow you to take out your expenses or running costs even though you may have paid for them in convertible pesetas. To safely ensure that there is no argument later about your initial importation of foreign currency, you should, at the time of importation, obtain a bank certificate verifying the amount you brought in.

The rest of your sale money will be held until it is established that you have no tax debts and that *plus valia* (capital gains) has been paid, if applicable. The price quoted on the *escritura* is usually lower than the actual selling price (see p66), and it is upon this figure that all taxes are assessed; do not try to be too clever because the authorities will investigate any ridiculous quote immediately – they will make their own assessment and charge the taxes on *their* figure, which may be above the price you are getting.

The one way that possibly you can help yourself is to get the buyer to pay part of the cost to you in sterling, outside Spain. To ensure the smooth running of such a transaction, either get him to give you a UK certified banker's cheque which you will immediately send to your UK bank, or get him to deposit the sum with your solicitor in the UK, to be credited to you on proof of sale. A photocopy of the first page of the *escritura* will do for this purpose, signed by both parties.

Please, *don't forget* that shady people do prey on the unwary – a whole separate book could be filled with the most alarming stories, of people ending up with no property and no money. The Spanish are pedantic, but if you do things correctly you are safe; but people do try to dodge paying taxes and fees, and it's a great temptation when you are talking about a total of 5 to 7 per cent of the purchase price if you are a purchaser, and almost an equal amount if you are selling, once you have paid agent's fees and capital gains tax. But don't be tempted, and if you are selling, make sure your purchaser either has the funds, by making him produce a certified cheque at the sale, or a banker's cheque if he is getting a mortgage. Once the deed is signed the property is his, and any shortfall is your loss.

If you are selling the property in order to purchase another in Spain you will not be liable to capital gains tax provided all of the sum you have gained from the sale is put into the new property within twelve months.

A novel idea is currently being tried by some Britishers who have found that the standstill in the UK housing market has left them unable to sell up and move out to Spain: they are advertising a swop of properties, British for Spanish. It sounds an excellent idea for both parties, but it is difficult to imagine how a Spanish tax official will cope with the notional value of a property in the UK as a base figure for his capital gains calculation. Not to mention the UK solicitor's dilemma with no selling price on which to calculate his fee!

Moving Back

The mechanics of the move back to the UK are somewhat like putting the 'moving out' chapter into reverse gear. You contact the company who moved your effects out, they will give you an estimate – you will probably once again decide to halve the list of things you could not leave behind and get another quote. A UK customs declaration form must be completed showing all items which may attract duty. It is wise to keep all receipts for electrical appliances and send photocopies only with the declaration. Provided you have been out of the UK for longer than a year and provided none of the items is under six months old, it is unlikely that the UK customs will levy any charges. If you have not got an address to go straight to in the UK the carriers will store your effects. However, this is a costly business nowadays so get quotes for storage from not only the carrier but other firms in the UK too – you could save a lot of money.

Children

If you have children it is better for them if you move during the long summer recess; they can then start at their UK school at the beginning of the academic year when new phases of the curriculum begin. Get the most detailed report you can from the child's school in Spain, including the syllabus being followed and any performance results in tests or exams. If the child is at the critical age of fourteen, a list of his subject options will be useful to the new school, as efforts can then be made to accommodate him without too many changes being made. All this information should be sent to the school of your choice or in the school in your catchment area as soon as possible, and an early appointment with the head teacher or year head should be sought after your arrival in the UK. It must be stressed that children returning from Spain will find things very different if they face going back into a large comprehensive school. Almost all English-speaking schools in Spain are run on lines similar to UK public schools with smaller classes and quite a lot of extra mural involvement, so do try to understand what the change must feel like to the child. A child that becomes withdrawn, or suddenly disruptive, may be trying to tell you something about his failure to adjust. School counsellors can be a great help in these circumstances.

Pets
If you are taking pets back to the UK do remember the quarantine laws, which require cats, dogs and similar mammals to be confined in an authorised kennel for a period of six months. This can be a very traumatic experience both for the animal and you; it is also a very expensive business, costing in the order of £700 for a cat and closer to £1,000 for a large dog. There are no options if you wish to keep the animal, and if you are foolish enough to try and smuggle it into the country the penalties are very severe. An alternative if your attachment to the animal isn't very strong is to leave it in the hands of a trusted friend in Spain. Many people contemplating return do advertise their pets in the English language newspapers and many find good homes. Really it is a matter of conscience, and your feelings of responsibility that finally win. By way of consolation many animal psychologists do claim that domestic animals will adjust quite happily to a fresh group of caring humans, so you might consider leaving your pet as the kinder option.

Cars
If you bought your car in the UK and paid the taxes on it, you are allowed to just drive it back and re-register it with the DVLC Swansea; nothing more is needed. If, however, you bought the car in the UK free of taxes you will be required to inform the VAT department who may

177

levy a percentage of the tax depending on how long you have owned it.

If you are taking a car back that was purchased in Spain or another country you will have to go through the importation procedure, and taxes may be levied. The rule is to take all receipts and documents relating to the ownership and purchase with you, and make particularly sure that any 'tax paid' element of the price is clearly shown.

As a word of warning, left-hand drive cars do attract a higher insurance premium in the UK and their second-hand value is far below that of a similar right-hand drive car, so if you plan on staying in the UK you would be advised to sell your left-hand drive car before leaving Spain where there is a better market for it.

If you want to be really clever, you can go to Belgium six months before you are due to leave Spain, purchase a right-hand drive car free of taxes, and then drive it back to the UK when you leave. It will work out a lot cheaper than the UK price even when you have paid the portion of the VAT due. However this trick will not work if you have a Spanish work permit or *residencia*.

Whatever car you take back, do make sure that you have an insurance policy which is valid for UK roads. Any British insurer will issue you with a cover note by post if you have completed a proposal form, and many UK insurers are established in Spain – Sun Alliance, Guardian Royal Exchange, etc – and they will always help on this point. Your no-claims bonus may also be transferable.

Well, that's dealt with going back – it's a jolly sight easier than coming out, but the shock comes with winter and the first fuel bills and the cost of winter lettuce and tomatoes, to say nothing of the peppers and the fruit. Oh dear, I hear you say, have we done the right thing? The paper says the temperature is 70°F (21°C) in Malaga today!

11

The Canary Islands

Whilst these islands are very much a part of Spain in that they share the same government, language and culture, they are separated from it by over 720 miles (1,160km) of sea and because of this enjoy considerable administrative autonomy.

The name 'Canaries' was given to the islands by early visitors who found that there were a great number of dogs to be found, and the name is derived from the Latin root for dog, *canis*. They were called the 'fortunate' or 'lucky islands' by the early Romans and this was indeed apt, for the Canaries enjoy one of the most hospitable climates one could find.

Geographically they are situated on a line with the Sahara Desert and close to the Tropic of Cancer, stretching between 27° and 29° south; this should make them unbearably hot for most of the year, but because they are 80 miles (129km) out in the Atlantic they benefit from the moderating effects of the gulf stream breezes which constantly play upon their shores. It is small wonder that they rapidly grew in popularity once the new lands of the Americas were opened; they also provided an ideal staging point for voyagers to gather water and provisions before starting the passage across the Atlantic.

The archipelago is thought to be volcanic in origin as it is formed near the chain of islands which extend from Iceland in the north to Tristan da Cunha in the south. There is ample evidence to support this theory, with many recently extinct volcanoes being present on the islands and a vast range of semi-volcanic material making up the soil base; black beaches are washed by Atlantic breakers, and hot sands, springs and geysers all point towards their geological formation millions of years ago.

The first visitors found a rather tall, fair race of people inhabiting the archipelago, whom some believed were descended from North African roots; the name given to them – *Guanche* – was thought to be derived from the combination of *guan* (man) with *achinch* (white mountain) which referred to Tenerife's snow-capped Mt Teide. The Guanche were a Stone Age people who worshipped the sun, and, it is said, so deeply revered women that once their honour was wounded only the death of the violator could satisfy.

The islands had many invaders through the early ages, and each time the Guanche put up a fierce opposition; however, during the reign of Henry III of Castile the islands of Hierro, Gunera, Lanzarote and Fuerteventura fell to the Spanish flag, to be followed by Gran Canaria and La Palma some years later. The final assault on Tenerife was made by Chevalier Alonso Fernadez de Lugo in 1494; he landed on the day of the Holy Cross and this name was given to the capital of the island, Santa Cruz. Spain therefore finally owned all the Canaries, but it was not the last fighting the islands would witness. Pirates attacked frequently; and in 1797 Tenerife was attacked by Nelson and it was there that he lost an arm.

Early Spanish settlers were encouraged to farm the fertile volcanic soils, and fishing communities netted vast catches to be salted and sent back to Spain. In this respect little has changed – the islands are one vast, semi-tropical garden, their crops are dispatched all over Europe and their fishing fleets harvest a generous sea.

Why the Canaries?

For the modern-day settler the island group presents one of the best options in terms of Spanish-owned territory. The islands enjoy a great deal of autonomy, and they are tax-free, thus removing much of the bureaucracy that puzzles and often infuriates the mainland settler. They do

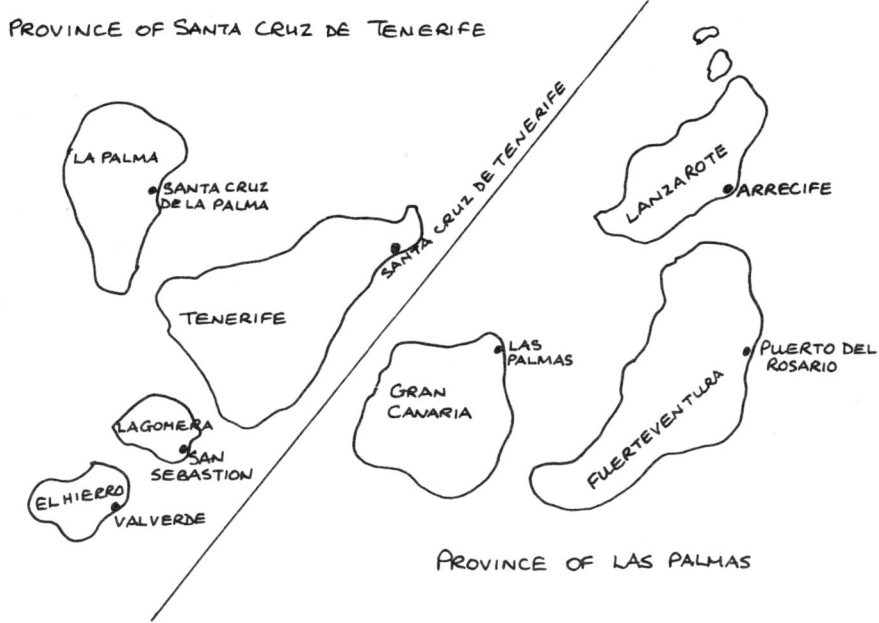

The Canary Islands

not have a winter; temperatures range from 59° to 86°F (15° to 30°C) throughout the year and there is quite enough rainfall to sustain the colourful garden-like appearance of many of the islands.

From a practical point of view it is farther from the UK than Spain and the cost of moving yourself and your effects will be initially higher; but once there you will find no IVA (VAT), no property tax, and no luxury goods tax. Thus you can buy many items like cars and electrical goods far more cheaply than in the UK or Spain – but don't forget to add the extra transport cost involved in getting any goods to the islands, as this certainly chops away at the overall saving.

Day-to-day living is cheaper than in Spain, and certainly cheaper than living in the UK. Fresh fruit and vegetables abound all the year round, and seafood of every kind is more reasonably priced. Because winter doesn't come there are none of its concomitant heating bills; the local water on most islands is good thanks to the absence of lime; and solar heating really is a viable alternative, after the initial shock of basic installation costs have been met.

Micro-climates abound in the island group, so you would do well to follow the practice of holidaying around before buying, or at least try renting for a year.

Property prices are on a par with the mainland, but do take care what you buy – get good legal advice, as much of the land is considered a military zone (*zona militaria*) and as such you require special dispensations to build – these may not have been obtained for the property you contemplate buying.

You will still be required to pay personal taxes on your world income and you will, of course, have to pay local rates and taxes, for whilst the Canary Islands are duty free, they still have an economy to manage.

One thing to keep in mind is that the tourist season never ends – if you are contemplating a business linked to tourism, good luck, it's a year-round earner. But if you plan to retire or stay permanently in a resort area remember it will never get quiet, so buy a property which is set back from the coastal strip so you can get some sleep.

Regular air services link the islands with each other and with the major cities in Spain and Europe, but return air fares do not enjoy a seasonal drop so you must be prepared to pay much the same price for your trip to the UK all the year round. Palma, Malaga and Alicante flight costs drop to just over £50 in winter if you shop around, whereas fares to Las Palmas or Tenerife seldom drop below £125 (1989 rates).

Finally, if you are planning on making the islands your home, try and get to know members of the English community who are already established there. Their information and views will be first-hand and up-to-date, and no book, no matter how well researched, can be that accurate.

Appendix 1
Useful Addresses

In the UK
The Spanish Consulate General
20, Draycott Place
London SW3 2RZ
(Very near Sloane Square)

The Spanish Consulate General
63 North Castle St
Edinburgh EH 3

Spanish Tourist Office
57/58 St James St
London SW1

The Spanish Chamber of Commerce
5 Cavendish Square
London W1M 0DP

The Spanish Commercial Office
22, Manchester Square
London W1M 5AR

The Spanish Institute
102 Eaton Square
London SW1

The Department of Health and Social Security
Long Benton
Newcastle NE98 1XY

HM Inspector of Taxes
Government Buildings
Ty Glas Rd
Llanshen
Cardiff CF4 5XS

Paymaster General's Office (Government Pensions)
Sutherland House
Russell Way
Crawley
West Sussex RH10 1UH

In Spain
All enquiries concerning the importation of any item
which may cause questions to be asked at the Spanish
border should be addressed to:

Direccion General de Aduanas
Guzman el Bueno 137
Madrid 28040

Sun Alliance Insurance SA
Compania Espania de Seguros
Tuset 20 24
Barcelona 08006

Recreation
Camping
Federacion Española de Empresarios de Camping
Calle Gran Via
88 Grupo 310 8
Madrid 28013

Golf
Real Federacion Española de Golf
Calle Captain Haya 9
Madrid

Fishing
ICONA
Avenida Gran Via de San Francisco 35
Madrid

Sailing and boating
Federacion Española de Vela
Calle Juan Vigon 23
Madrid

Appendix 1: Useful Addresses

Diving
Federacion Espanola de Actividades Subacuaticos
Calle Santalo 15
Barcelona

Skiing
Federacion Española de Deportes Invierno
Calle Claudio Coello 32
Madrid

British Consulates in Spain
Alicante
Calvo Sotelo 1–2
Alicante 1
Tel: (952) 521 61 90

Barcelona
Avenida Generalissimo Franco 477
(Piso 13) Barcelona 11
Tel: (3) 322 21 51

Balearics
Plaza Mayor
Palma de Mallorca
Tel: 71 24 45

Madrid
Calle de Fernañdo el Santo 16
Madrid 4
Tel: (1) 419 02 00

Malaga
Duquesa de Parchant 8
Tel: (952) 21 75 71

National Association of British Schools in Spain

This is just a selection from amongst the English-speaking schools throughout Spain which are approved by the National Association. Should your intended area not be shown in the list, a letter to the nearest school will provide you with all the information you should require concerning other schools registered within the organisation

Town and address of school	*Educational level Age range (No on roll)*
Marbella: Alona College El Angel Nueva Andelucia Marbella	GCSE + A level 3 to 17 (390)
Baleares: Baleares International School Calle Cabo Mateu coch 17 San Agustin Palma de Mallorca	GCSE + A level 4 to 16 (230)
Gran Canaria: British School of Gran Canaria Aparto 11 Tafira Alta Las Palmas Gran Canaria	GCSE + O level 4 to 16 (300)
Lanzarote: British School of Lanzarote José Antonio 80 Arrecife	4 to 14 (130)
Valencia: Cambridge House Campo Olivar 40110 Valencia	3 to 11 (110)

Appendix 1: Useful Addresses

Barcelona:
The Anglo-American School
Paseo de Garbi 152
08033 Castell de Fels
Barcelona

GCSE + A level
3 to 18   (240)

Tenerife:
British Yeoward School
Parque Tacro 30440
Puerto de la Cruz
Tenerife

3 to 16   (265)

Madrid:
King's College
Paseo de los Andes
s/n Soto de Vinuelas
28770 Colmenar Viejo
Madrid

GCSE + A level
3 to 19   (930)

Cadiz:
International School of Sotogrande
Apartado 15
11130 Sotogrande
Cadiz

GCSE + O level
3 to 16   (230)

Torremolinos:
Sunny View School
Cerro de Toril Apt 175
29620 Torremolinos
Malaga

GCSE + A level
4 to 18   (350)

Alicante:
Sierra Bernia School
La Caneta San Rafael
03580 Alfaz del Pi
Alicante

GCSE + A level
3 to 18   (160)

Fuengirola:
St Anthony's College
Avenida Alcapulco
Los Boliches Apt 9
29050 Fuengirola

GCSE + A level
3 to 18   (250)

English Language Churches
The Diocese of Gibraltar in Europe
Bishop:
The Rt Rev John R Satterthwaite
Diocesan Office
5a Gregory Place
London W8 4NG

Barcelona:
St George's
Calle San Juan de la Salle 41
Horacio 38
22 Barcelona

Costa Blanca:
Rev R.E. Hicks
Apt 242, Altea
Alicante
(For service times, see the *Costa Blanca News*)

Costa del Sol East:
Rev R.S. Matheson
Chaplaincy House
Calle los Naranjos 17
Pueblo Lopez
Fuengirola

Costa del Sol West:
Rev S.L. Elkington
Casa 3 1b
Edificio Ben Azur
Urban el Pilar
Estepona
Malaga

Madrid:
St George
Nunez de Balboa 43
Madrid

Malaga:
St George
Avenida de Pries
Malaga

Palma and the Balearics:
St Philip and St James
Calle Nunez de Balboa 6
Son Armadams
Palma de Mallorca

The Spanish Reformed Episcopal Church:
Rt Rev Arturo Sandiez
Calle de Beneficencia 18
Madrid

Church of Scotland in Europe:
121, George St
Edinburgh EH2 4YN

The Methodist Church in Europe:
Area Secretary for Europe
Methodist Church Overseas Division
25, Marylebone Rd
London NW1 5JR

Appendix 2
Shopping Glossary

This is a brief guide to the names of shops and an idea of what they sell. It becomes a bit confusing to the shopper when he asks where they sell a tap washer or broom and he's told to look for the *ferreteria*, so read on and discover the mystery of the shop signs.

butcher	*carniceria*
car hire	*alquilar coches*
cosmetics, soaps, shampoos etc	*drogaria*
dentist	*dentista*
dispensing chemist	*farmacia*
DIY goods	*bricolaje*
dry cleaners and laundry	*tintoria/lavanderia*
estate agents	*inmobiliaria*
fish shop	*pescadaria*
food shop	*tienda comestibles*
garden centre	*centro jardin*
hairdressing salon	*peluqueria*
hypermarket	*hipermercado*
imported foods	*tienda ultramarinos*
iron mongers and DIY	*ferreteria*
library	*biblioteca*
medical clinic	*centro medico*
money changing	*cambio*
old name for tobacconist's	*estanco*
opticians	*centro optico*
papers and magazines	*periodicos y revistas*
perfumes and cosmetics	*perfumaria*
photographers	*fotografia*
plumber's fitments	*fontanaria*

police HQ	*comisaria*
Red Cross	*cruz roja*
shop	*tienda*
supermarket	*supermercado*
tobacco, stamps, cards etc	*tabacaleria*
wine bar	*bodega*
wood and DIY	*carpenteria*

Food Shopping
Beef (ternera)

fillet steak	*solomillo*
stewing meat	*carne para estofados*
liver	*higado*
veal	*ternera blanca*

Lamb (cordero)

leg	*pierna*
shoulder	*brazo*
chops	*chuletas*
kidneys	*rinones*
mutton	*lanar mayor*

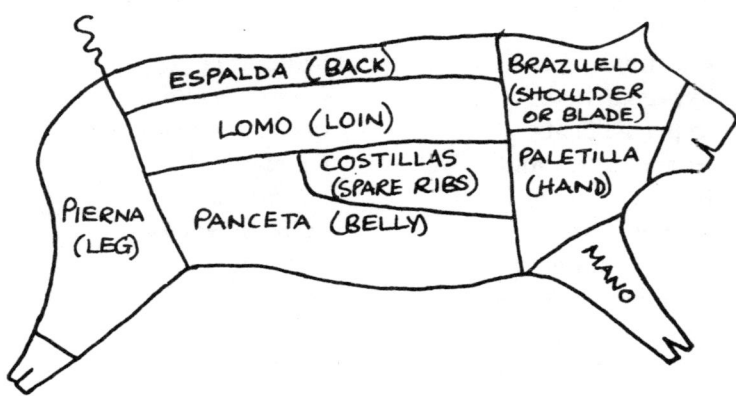

Pork cuts (cerdo)

Pork (cerdo)

boned leg cuts	*magra*
loin	*lomo*
ribs	*costillas*
belly	*panceta*
suckling pig	*lechona*

Poultry (aves)

chicken	*pollo*
free-range chicken	*pollo campero*
breast	*pechuga de pollo*
drumsticks	*muslitos*
hen	*gallina*
turkey	*pavo*
duck	*pato*

Shellfish (mariscos)

prawns	*langostinos*
shrimps	*gambas*
mussels	*mejillones*
clams	*almejas*
crabs	*cangrejos*

Fish (pescado)

hake	*merluza*
red sea bream	*pageles*
sardines	*sardinas*
anchovies	*boqueron*
cod	*bacalao*
mackerel	*caballa*
trout	*trucha*
bass	*lubina*
tuna	*atun*
squid	*calamar*
octopus	*pulpo*

Vegetables (verduras)

artichokes	*alcachofas*
asparagus	*esparragos*
aubergines	*berenjenas*

beetroot	*remolacha*
broad beans	*habas*
Brussels sprouts	*coles de bruselas*
carrots	*zanahorias*
cress	*berros*
cucumber	*pepino*
garlic	*ajo*
green beans	*judias verde*
green peppers	*pimientos verdes*
lettuce	*lechuga*
mushrooms	*championes*
onions	*cebollas*
parsley	*perejil*
peas	*guisantes*
potatoes	*patatas*
radishes	*rabanos*
red peppers	*pimientos rojos*
spinach	*espinacas*

Fruit (fruitas)

apples	*manzanas*
avocado	*aguacates*
bananas	*platanos*
grapefruit	*pomelo*
grapes	*uvas*
lemons	*limones*
melon	*melon*
oranges	*naranjas*
pears	*peras*
pineapples	*pinas*
plums	*ciruelas*
peaches	*melocotons*
strawberries	*fresas*
water melon	*sandia*

Clothing Sizes (*tallas*)
Note: as in other countries, sizes do vary with the manufacturer.

Ladies' (*mujeres*)	UK	Spain
Dresses, blouses, suits		
(*Vestidos, camisas, trajes*)	10	40
	12	42
	14	44
	16	46
	18	48

Men's (*hombres*)		
Shirts (*camisas*)	14	36
	14½	37
	15	38
	15½	39
	16	40
	16½	41

Trousers (*pantalones*)		
	28/24	71/61
	30/26	76/66
	32/28	81/71
	34/30	86/76
	36/32	91/81

Shoes (*zapatos*)		
Adults:	4	37
	5	38
	6	39
	7	40
	8	42
	9	43
	10	45
	11	47

May I try it/them on? (*Puedo probarmelo?*) poo-ay-dho pro-bar-may-lo

Cheques, Bills and Bank Statements

Reading Your Bank Statement

Statement of your account

ESTADO DE SU CUENTA

(BB) BANCO DE BILBAO

DATOS DE LA CUENTA
Your account number

Siguiendo sus deseos, nos complace facilitar el movimiento solicitado de su cuenta

Fecha de Operación Date-Code	Clave	DEBE Debits	HABER Credits	Value Valoración date	SALDO Balance
		Saldo mayo 1988			22.400,00
26.5		20.000,00		23.5	2.400,00
29.5			10.400,00	26.5	12.800,00
30.5		6,000,00		27.5	6.800,00

You will observe that a full stop divides figures groups and a comma is a decimal point: thus the English 10,500.20 becomes 10.500,20

BB 860118 - E

Mod. 2 134

CLAVES DE OPERACION
DEBITOS
TA Talones de efectivo
      (2 últimas cifras)
TC Talones compensados
      (2 últimas cifras)
TV Talones de "varios"
      (2 últimas cifras)
1   Giros y transferencias.
3   Efectos recogidos.

5   Devoluciones
7   Gastos liquidación remesas.
9   Recibos domiciliados.
11 Seguros Sociales.
15 Reintegros.
21 Compra de valores.
23 Suscripciones, Dividendos pasivos.
33 Operaciones de extranjero.
43 Efec. recogidos - Cámara.
55 Gastos o comisiones.

65 Banco 24 horas.
67 Créditos personales.
69 Tarjeta de crédito.
77 Intereses a su cargo.
87 Otros conceptos.
ABONOS
10 Abonarés de compensación.
20 Ingresos en efectivo.
24 Banco 24 horas.
30 Transferencias y órdenes a su favor.

40 Remesas de efectos.
50 Venta de valores.
60 Cupones.
68 Créditos personales.
70 Operaciones de extranjero.
80 Intereses a su favor.
88 Operaciones varias.

DEBITOS O ABONOS

90 Anulaciones - Correcciones.

196

How to Read Your Electric Bill

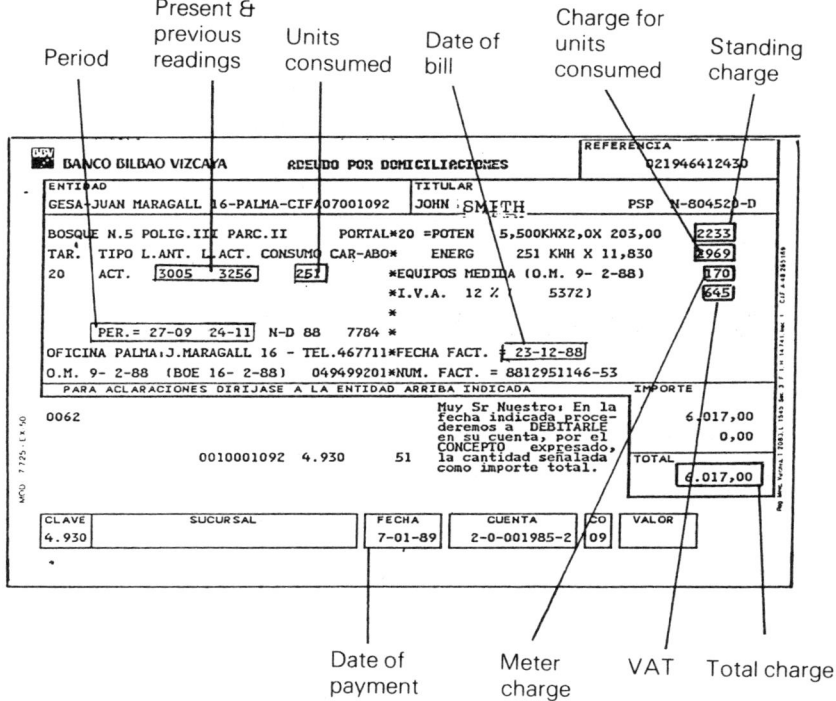

Period

Present & previous readings

Units consumed

Date of bill

Charge for units consumed

Standing charge

Date of payment

Meter charge

VAT

Total charge

Making Out a Spanish Cheque

Index

Index